The Politics of Memory

The Politics of Memory

THE JOURNEY OF A HOLOCAUST HISTORIAN

Raul Hilberg

Chicago · Ivan R. Dee

Library of Congress Cataloging in-Publication Data:
Hilberg, Raul, 1926–
The politics of memory : the journey of a Holocaust historian /
Raul Hilberg.
p.   cm.
Includes index.
ISBN 1-56663-428-8
1. Hilberg, Raul, 1926–   . 2. Holocaust, Jewish
(1939–1945)—Historiography. 3. Jewish historians—
United States—Biography.
I. Title.
D804.348.H55   1996   96-11953
940.53'18—dc20

Preface

MUCH OF MY LIFE has been devoted to the study of a subject that in fundamental ways is different from any other: the destruction of the European Jews. Often enough, acquaintances as well as strangers have wanted to know why I undertook such an exploration and what sort of reactions I encountered in the course of my work. In this account of my experiences I have consolidated and elaborated my answers to these questions. The result is a personal story but one which touches upon a range of phenomena that are part and parcel of the politics of memory in America, Israel, and Europe from the late 1940s to the early 1990s.

I have shared drafts of these pages with my old friend Eric Marder, my longtime literary agent Theron Raines, my newly found kindred spirit Walter Reich, my wife Gwendolyn, my son David, and my daughter Deborah. Each approached the manuscript with special perspectives, and from all I received valuable insights and suggestions. I thank them for everything they have given me.

Contents

History without tragedy does not exist,

and knowledge is better and more wholesome

than ignorance.

—H. G. Adler

The Politics of Memory

I
The Review

ON TUESDAY, SEPTEMBER 15, 1992, I received a call from my literary agent Theron Raines, a man of learning who was born in Arkansas and who earned degrees at Columbia College and Oxford University. Raines is always to the point, always clear. My new book, he said, was going to be reviewed on the following Sunday in the *New York Times*. I thanked him for the call, but in a relaxed manner as if to suggest that I was now at an age when such news was not about to make me euphoric. Still, I was pleased. I no longer had any professional enemies who might want to tear me down in print. Consequently there was everything to look forward to and nothing to fear. But then, Theron Raines added, "You are not going to like the last sentence of the review."

That evening my wife brought home facsimile copies of two reviews sent to her office by my editor at Harper-Collins, Aaron Asher. The review in the *New York Times* was one of them. I read both quickly and decided to put them aside, because my daughter was visiting me and I did not wish to spoil our time together. On Sunday I would leave for a book tour, starting in Boston, and she would return to Jerusalem. Aaron Asher, however, was worried. He called me on Thursday and asked whether the two reviews, particularly the one in the *Times*, should be answered. My immediate reply was no, because these were sophisticated discussions, and I did not wish to refute them. He countered that in the *Times* I had been accused of lack of scholarship. True, I said, in a manner of speaking my research had been found wanting, but still I did not wish to write a letter.

I knew the reviewer in the *Times* personally. He had invited me to lecture at his university and had written glowingly about the second edition of my large book, *The Destruction of the European Jews*, in the London *Times Literary Supplement*. Now he not only dismissed my new study but revised his thoughts about the second edition of the earlier work. In his reevaluation he was reviewing my whole life, starting with the first edition of *Destruction* published more than thirty years before. He praised *that* edition and asked pointedly, "What does one do when such a work is completed?" He explained that I had taught political science at the University of Vermont until my retirement; I had inspired a new generation, serving as mentor and guide. When the second edition of *Destruction* was published in 1985, reviewers had paid homage to my "original achievement," but some were "disappointed" with the new version. Finally, in my new book, *Perpetrators Victims Bystanders*, I had remained "aloof" from younger scholars who had created new work with new documentation and new questions. I had become, he said in his last sentence, "less a pathfinder than a conscience."

Always in my life I had wanted the truth about myself. Here was an assessment by a man who was in no sense ignorant and who bore me no ill will. What if he were right? When I first embarked upon my self-imposed task at the age of twenty-two, I was working alone, trying to grapple with my enormous topic which stood for the epitome of human destruction in our time. I had immersed myself in this history, delving deeper and deeper into the documents of the German bureaucracy of the Nazi era in an attempt to touch bottom. I was thirty-five when my first word on the subject appeared in print. What had I done in the last thirty-one years? What had happened to me?

I shared the review with my old friend Eric Marder. It was not so bad, he said, considering the flattering sentences in those paragraphs devoted to my early accomplishments. I asked him to read the whole review over again, assuring him that I myself had studied it five times before its full impact was clear to me. He called me back after he too had read the review five times. It was not so good, he confirmed, but to him the real question was, Why should I accept the premises of this reviewer? Why should I agree with these conclusions? I countered with the argument that, above all, I had to remain clear-sighted. Never had I tried to delude myself, and now especially the truth was most important to me. Perhaps my creative potential had been exhausted three decades ago. Conceivably I had lingered on this earth since then.

Yet I was not completely sure. When I had completed the new work, with its focus on people rather than events, I had shipped it without mental reservations to Theron Raines. At HarperCollins, Aaron Asher had read the manuscript and accepted it without hesitation. It was still early;

the book was just on its way to the stores. Why not wait? Although the footnotes had been banished to the back of the book, they were not lost, and someone might call attention to the variety of my sources. If, as Eric suggested and my son believed, the book was too subtle, another reviewer might nonetheless discover its intricacy. As for sales, major stores might have piled up copies for strollers wandering through the aisles.

On the Sunday morning of September 20, I boarded a plane to Boston. It was still morning when I arrived. I bought a copy of the *Boston Globe*, in which I had once reviewed a book, but it was silent. I visited the large Barnes & Noble store—the only bookshop open before noon—but the book was not there. In American politics there are election nights when a candidate, fighting for survival, awaits the result of a vote in a single crucial precinct, because a negative outcome there signifies the loss of the entire contest. For me, Boston was such a test.

I returned to the hotel for my lunch in a dining room just above the street-level restaurant The Last Hurrah. The food was unexpectedly good, and even more excellent was the guitarist whose sounds filled the room. I listened to his masterful playing of Francisco Tarrega's *Recuerdos de la Alhambra*. Suddenly I felt an indescribable sadness. So this is the end, the real end, regardless of what may still happen. That moment I was alone with myself, saying goodbye to my life.

II
Background

Origins

MY FATHER ONCE TOLD ME that even before I was born I was sufficiently unruly to cause a serious problem for my mother, and that in the hospital he was asked by the obstetrician whether, in the event of a dilemma necessitating a choice between the survival of my mother and the life of the child, he would prefer the one or the other. At that moment—so he confided to me—he made a decision that was wholly inappropriate in the light of all the teachings of the sages, but that was nevertheless compelling in his eyes. In such an eventuality, he told the physician, it was my life he wanted saved. This secret he shared with me while I was still a schoolboy, in one of the conversations we had about his own childhood and his adolescence, employment, and military service. I was impressed with all his accounts, and I have always thought of my father as a wise and considerate man. To me he was a guide from whom I have tried, not always successfully, to draw my ideas, attitudes, and style.

There was a vast difference between my father, who had experienced and suffered much, and my mother, who did survive my arrival. It is difficult to talk about them in the same paragraph or on the same page, and so I will begin by describing them separately.

My father was born on September 15, 1889, in what he remembered as an unpaved village in the northeastern part of the Austro-Hungarian Empire: Dzuryn (or transliterated from the Russian: Dzhurin). Much later I looked up the place, which is now located in the western portion of Ukraine, and found it clearly visible on a good map. It had evidently become a town, considerably larger than I had expected. The Hilbergs, my father said, had come to Dzuryn from Bavaria in 1648, but I did not verify this information. One Hilberg, perhaps a cousin of my paternal grandfather, was a rector of the University of Czernowitz (subsequently Cernauti and thereafter Chernovtsy) sometime before the First World War. Considering the utterly humble circumstances of my father's extended family, I always thought the story of the successful Hilberg to be apocryphal, but searching at one time in a library catalog of Southern Methodist University for cards with titles of my own literary output, I discovered that the Hilberg of Czernowitz was real, and that he had written several books on such subjects as the formation of syllables in ancient Greek. From then on I resolved never to disbelieve anything my father had told me.

My father left Dzuryn shortly after he had completed his schooling at about the age of fourteen. Europe was still at peace, optimism reigned, and choices could be made with an expectation of improving one's life. He told me that he had visited Zurich and Berlin before settling in Vienna. Because I was still very young, it did not occur to me to ask him whether his travel was financed by his parents. They must have been very poor, because my father never gave me any details about the occupation of my grandfather. In fact, he did not say very much about him altogether. All I heard was the story of my grandfather's flight from the advancing Russian army in the First World War and his death during that war as a refugee.

My father, one of ten children, had a living sister and three living brothers, the usual residue from deaths in infancy. The oldest brother and the only sister lived in New York, where they too were poor. A younger brother, Josef, followed my father to Vienna. My father was heavily preoccupied with Josef, and after Josef's death with his memory. Josef was a man who left no mark at all. He was dependent on my father immediately on his arrival in Vienna. During the First World War he pretended to have a bad leg, and limped throughout the four years of the conflict. So successful was Josef in this act of draft evasion that he had trouble resuming a normal gait after Austria's defeat. He was childless, and his tiny apartment, in which he lived with his wife, was not even suited for the briefest visitor. I always hated to go there, for I stood in the middle of the small living room, which was also the bedroom, where I had to listen to his sighs about the terrible state of the economy and his unending hardships. After Vienna became a part of the German Reich, Josef crossed the Belgian border illegally and fled again in 1940, to be interned in a camp where stateless and stranded people just like Josef and his wife were held by the collaborationist French Vichy regime. My father, by then in New York, received Josef's frantic appeals for help, but there was no money for tickets which might have enabled Josef to escape to America. When the deportations from the Vichy-French zone began in 1942, Josef disappeared. "The blood of my brother is upon me," my father would say at that time, and years later he repeated these words to signify that this failure to pay for the berths on a ship was his greatest sin, never to be expiated. In 1978 I looked for Josef on a list of deportees from France. There was no record of a Josef Hilberg. How invisible could a man be? Then it occurred to me that my grandparents had been married only in a religious ceremony, and if Josef had not taken formal steps to change his name he would have had to carry the maiden name of my grandmother, Gaber, on his personal documents. Although the postwar French transcribers of the deportation lists had trouble deciphering some of the original entries, I found Gaber, Joseph, born October 23, 1893, in "Dzwyen." He was deported on August 14, 1942, and arrived in Auschwitz two days later. Since he was already forty-eight years old, he must have been gassed immediately.

Unlike Josef, my paternal uncle Jakob was a soldier in the First World War. As an artilleryman he fired heavy Austrian shells in support of German forces on the Western front. Although never wounded, Jakob returned from the war half deaf. He never left Poland again, and I never met him, his wife, or their children. The German occupants of Poland in the Second World War, I must surmise, thanked him for his help by killing him and his family.

All my knowledge about my paternal grandmother comes from my father, and all he really told me about her concerned her extreme pacifism. When he was discharged from a military hospital and visited her in Dzuryn after the war, she burned all his uniforms and papers, and threw away all his medals. She overlooked only a creased photograph which shows him as a sergeant in the Austro-Hungarian army. By 1942, in her eighties and blind, she lay in bed most of the time. Apparently that is where the German raiders found her and where they shot her on the spot.

I could understand how a woman with two sons at the front could have become peace-loving. What I could not grasp so easily was my father's description of himself as a pacifist. War, he said, is not what the chauvinists and romantics write about it. He had spent twenty-six months in the trenches, twenty-two months on the Russian front, and, after being wounded in the neck, four more months on the Italian front, where a shell smashed his shinbone and left him in the hospital with gangrene. But, I interjected, he had also been decorated. His silver medal, as I learned later, was at least the equivalent of an Iron Cross First Class in the German army or a Silver Star in the American army. True, he would answer, but what had he received these decorations for? Once he rescued a major, whose guts had been ripped out. Another time he had to repair a torn wire of the Austrian telephone lines at night. Losing his way, he hooked it up by mistake with a Russian wire. Since he understood Russian, he overheard a conversation signaling an attack on a regimental front to begin at dawn. He was going back, he thought, as he came, but lost his way again and arrived at a neighboring German regiment from which he called his colonel, Herrn Oberst von Wipplinger. "Do you know what you are saying?" the colonel asked him. "If you are right I must withdraw the entire regiment to the reserve trench, the B-Line, and if you are wrong . . ." The Austrians withdrew and for several hours the Russians bombarded an empty trench. When Russian infantry began their assault, the Austrians filtered back into their old positions. The first Russian wave collapsed in no-man's-land, and the second barely reached the Austrian line. The third turned back in flight. That is what he had gotten one of his medals for: three thousand Russian dead as a result of his inability to orient himself on the ground.

No, he was a pacifist, and he served for only one reason: honor. Jewish honor. For this attitude he could give a concrete example. Once he led a patrol into no-man's-land where he was suddenly confronted by an enemy patrol. The Russians, however, were just as surprised. He addressed the Russian patrol leader quickly and discovered that in both patrols there were several Jews. They decided not to fight but to talk. Sitting in a shell hole, they traded alcohol and food—the Austrians had the rum and the Russians the bread. At the end of this meeting my father said to his Russian counterpart, who was also Jewish, "Alcohol is prohibited in your army; come, surrender to us and you will drink." The Russian replied, "No, you are starving in your army; come, surrender to us and you will eat." Inasmuch, however, as both sergeants were men of honor, they bid each other goodbye, and each returned to his own lines to continue the war.

When my father returned to Vienna he had to build his life anew. His first task was to walk. Lying in the hospital, he overheard a military doctor remark to a colleague that he was not likely to live. Then an Austrian surgeon inserted a silver shinbone in my father's leg. The Austrians gave him crutches, assuring him that he would need them for the rest of his days. After some months my father discarded the crutches and walked with a cane. Then he put aside the cane and simply walked. While he was still crippled, the postwar Austrian government asked him whether he wanted to avail himself of a tiny pension or an income tax deduction for his disability. When he chose the deduction, the bureaucrats laughed. He persisted, even though an older partner in the minuscule business they had founded before the war had become bankrupt while my father was at the front, and even after the economic depression of the 1930s dealt him a further blow. He had my mother and he had me, and his life seemed fulfilled.

Not so fulfilled, it seems, was my mother's life. Recapitulating her experience is a problem. Although I spent much more time in my childhood with her than with my father, I do not recall any real conversations we may have had. I could learn something about her only by asking repeated questions about her childhood and family, and even then her disclosures were sometimes incomplete or misleading. She claimed that her original home was in Buczacz, a city in Galicia, also in the northeastern corner of the Austro-Hungarian Empire. Buczacz, I heard, was important enough to have a *Gymnasium*, the sort of school that was a stepping-stone to higher education in a college or university. Much later, however, I learned that she was actually born and raised in the insignificant village of Podzameczek, which is adjacent to Buczacz but clearly separated from it by the river Strypa. In describing her extended family, she was most prepared to talk about one individual, Naphtali Herz Imber, who was related to my maternal grandmother, and who is immortalized in the *Encyclopedia Judaica* as the poet responsible for the words of Israel's national anthem, the Ha-Tikvah, or "The Hope." For many years I had assumed that he had composed the music as well—"He wrote the Ha-Tikvah," my mother had said—but the *Encyclopedia* corrected my misapprehension. The famous Imber had written only the words. Moreover, they were derived in part from the Polish anthem "Poland Is Not Yet Lost."

My mother was one of eighteen siblings, half of whom survived their infancy. Her oldest brother, a promising classicist, died of an infection following a tooth extraction before the First World War. Most of the other brothers and sisters, who were older than my mother, had migrated to the United States. In Europe I knew my aunt, Augusta Szigeti, who lived in Sighet, Romania, with her son Alexander. Augusta, who manufactured violins, had much more money than we. She owned a house and garden and was driven by a chauffeur in a Mercedes-Benz. In March 1939, as the war clouds gathered, Alexander, who was known as Sanyi, traveled to the Middle East, including Palestine. He was in his early twenties then, already mustered out of the Romanian army, in which he had performed his obligatory duty, and I thought that his trip was an exploration to determine whether the Holy Land was as hospitable and livable as his own Romania. Sanyi returned, possibly dissatisfied with his discoveries. He was already an expert in fine living, and I was particularly impressed with his taste in women.

Although I was only eleven when I saw him in Prague, I was awestruck by a young lady he escorted there. I am sure she was Jewish, but she looked almost Japanese to me, and very beautiful. I had an infatuation then with all manner of things Japanese—no doubt influenced by my father, who told me that during the Russo-Japanese War the Jews of Austria-Hungary, thinking of their oppressed brethren in Russia, had prayed fervently for a Japanese victory. Sanyi at any rate did not marry this woman but, as I heard after the war, another who, I hope, was no less beautiful. The couple had a little son before Augusta, Sanyi, and his family were swept up by the deportations to Auschwitz in the spring of 1944. There they disappeared into the night.

My mother had one younger brother, Heinrich, who was born at the turn of the century and who was an officer candidate in the Austro-Hungarian army before it collapsed in 1918. His uniformed service was not completed, however. He served as a lieutenant in the Polish army, fighting the Bolsheviks, and after that war he was a Polish captain of artillery in the reserve. This military career is remarkable because Heinrich had become a physician without relinquishing his status as an artillery officer. He lived in Gdynia on the Baltic coast, and I saw him only once, when he visited us in Vienna. To my great regret I never met his family. I still have a small photograph of his two daughters, which they sent me, addressed to *den lieben Raul*, and I studied it for a long time, concentrating on the older Sziutka, a handsome teenager. I do not know precisely what happened to Heinrich. From my mother I heard that sometime between September 1939 and June 1941 he was supposed to have been in Soviet-occupied Lvov. That is where the trail ended. No further word was received about him, his wife, or Sziutka and her little sister.

Only one aunt had remained in the Buczacz area, but for decades I barely knew that she existed. Her name was Frieda. My mother was reluctant to divulge anything about her. After persistent questioning I found that Frieda had been divorced. That is why nothing more could be said about her life. She too vanished in the 1940s during the German occupation of Poland.

My mother was far less reticent to talk about her father. She was already in her seventies when she visited me once in Vermont and revealed how much she had suffered in his house. Her troubles began when she was a sensitive girl, about thirteen years old. At that time her mother had died and her father, without waiting a year, had remarried. "Really?" I asked as I brewed tea for both of us. "Yes," she said, "that is what he did to me. So now you know." My grandfather, I must add for the record, also died in Adolf Hitler's Europe.

So unhappy was my mother in the northeastern part of the Austro-Hungarian Empire that she left it—I do not know exactly when—to live in Vienna, where, at last content, she became a bookkeeper, and where, at the age of twenty-six, she met my father. "Why did you marry him?" I would ask her. "I do not know," she would answer in an irritated voice. "I was influenced by friends who told me that I should." True, true, I said to myself, that would have been the advice to a woman who was not attracted to a man. Tens of thousands of Jewish soldiers had been killed in the Aus-

tro-Hungarian army, and many a young Jewish woman was
consigned to spinsterhood. It must have been my father
who was the pursuer. My supposition was confirmed after
her death, when I inherited her collection of family photographs. Among dozens of portraits of my uncle, the classicist who died after a visit to his dentist before the First
World War, I retrieved a photograph of my mother that she
had given to my father. Here she was in the glow of her
youth, yet stately, at the edge of that maturity which charac-
terizes a woman who already knows how to dress, move,
and pose. "Your mother was an attractive woman," my reli-
able father had told me. She was not as beautiful as Augusta,
whose face was almost blinding, but . . . He wanted my
mother, really wanted her, I concluded after I read a brief
notation on the back of her photograph. She had written
only two words, "*Bitte wenden*" (Please turn), and he had
added, evidently after she had agreed to become his wife,
"*veni, vidi, vici,*" the only brash words he had ever permitted
himself.

One should think that three people in a very modest
apartment would constitute a closely knit family, but in retrospect I realize that I spent time with my father and with
my mother, but not so much with them both simultaneously. Although my father habitually returned home midday
for his major meal, I do not recall any conversations between them. Subjects they deemed inappropriate for my
ears were in any case discussed in Polish, a language both of
them had mastered in childhood. Yet on a few occasions,
while speaking in German, a disagreement between them
welled into an argument, always initiated by my mother,

who would shout, *"Du bist ein Niemand!"* (You are a no-body!). It was the one expression my father did not accept with equanimity. His principal pride in life was his self-sufficiency. This accomplishment was not minor, and if he did not demand verbal recognition, still he could not ignore her outburst, which he answered with the assertion that he was certainly not a nobody. In her reply to this rejoinder, she called him Count Potocki—an allusion to the seven-teenth-century Polish lord who had granted privileges to the Jews of Buczacz.

Their exchanges made a lasting impression on me. I was convinced of my father's sense of worth, and I adopted his values, but I could not miss the undertone of my mother's message that he had fallen short, that she had been short-changed by her marriage, and that she deserved better. Thus, even while agreeing with him, I resolved to be better armed. Meanwhile my father did not help me when I tried to take his side, because then he would say that my mother had always done her duty. She was a superb cook, kept the house immaculately clean—albeit with the help of a house-keeper—and, above all, took very good care of me.

Only once did I overhear my mother defend my father. It was in November 1938, just after my father had been ar-rested in a major roundup of Jews, when a man with a pistol aimed straight at my mother demanded that we vacate the apartment at once. The Jews, he screamed, had always ex-ploited the German people, cheating them of their earnings and wealth. At this moment my mother replied calmly that my father had always worked honestly and that he had never broken the law.

My father was not kept under arrest very long. He had presence of mind, and when he noticed a "D" next to his name on a list, he quickly surmised that he was destined for the concentration camp Dachau. "Gentlemen, you cannot do that," he said politely to the two Gestapo men sitting behind a table. "Oh, we can't?" they answered. "No," he insisted, "I fought in the World War." "One moment, you Jew, where did you fight?" My father recited regimental locations. "We cannot send him to Dachau," said the older of the two Gestapo men. "He is not lying. I was there myself."

My father was released, but he was a broken man. He had not been tortured, and he was reunited with us in an apartment of friends who had taken us in. From this moment, however, he lost his independence. His business had been that of a middleman. It consisted of buying household goods for people who needed credit and who paid him in installments. In 1938 and 1939 the Aryan or Aryanized stores demanded all the money owed to them by Jews, but many of my father's customers could not or would not pay off their debts to him. Finally, it was my mother's family in the United States that enabled us to emigrate, and when my father and mother arrived in New York in 1940, both of them became factory workers. That was when my father concluded that he no longer had any say or claim in family matters. He had been robbed of his principal attainment, and henceforth he deferred to my mother for all those decisions still to be made. The issues, to be sure, had been narrowed considerably. Money had to be saved, dollar by dollar, and my father took as little as possible from the till. He was keenly interested in Israel, but he never went there, even after his retirement. Although he would have been more generous than my mother in allowing me to work fewer hours in a factory while I was still in college, or to forgive my monetary debt, which I accrued in later years by living in my parents' New York apartment, and which I calculated to be a third of the household cost for the time that I spent there after my sixteenth birthday, he never insisted that I be given any concessions. He had promised my mother in the early 1920s that she would never have to work, and in their middle age he could no longer keep his word.

My mother took good care of him when he became old. When they were both retired with social security benefits, she also had a small pension and he received a monthly check of approximately ten dollars paid to him by the Austrian government in recognition of his physical impairment resulting from his service in the First World War. My mother had time to watch his diet of pot cheese and assorted foods recommended for people with a heart condition, and he read books, which he selected not so much from the works of his beloved Heinrich Heine or even the biblical commentaries as from a club offering adventure novels in digest form. His life became narrower and narrower, and one day I was summoned from Vermont to see him for the last time. "He did not make it," the surgeon announced after my father had succumbed to a heavy dose of anesthesia. At that moment my mother burst into tears.

Formative Years

OUR APARTMENT IN VIENNA consisted of four rooms. I was told that at first it was shared with a previous tenant, an elderly gentleman, who died in due time. The rooms had higher ceilings than those to which Americans are accustomed, and they were relatively spacious. One of them, however, the foyer, was half filled by a large white linen closet in which my father stored goods for sale. By contrast, the living room furniture was all black, including the glassed bookcase which housed the works of Goethe, Heine, and Dostoevsky, as well as those of the Jewish historian Heinrich Graetz. This is the room I remember the most, and to this day I am partial to black, including black book covers and book jackets. Our furniture, like the house, was made to last for generations. In 1938, when we sold it, some of these pieces were purchased by the people who had ejected us.

Lest there be a mistaken impression about our comforts, I should emphasize that there was no running water in the apartment. A single spigot in the hallway served the entire floor. The toilets, one for each family, had separate doors in the hallway as well. The entrance to the house was a narrow corridor, and the spiral staircase was made of stone. We had an icebox, a telephone, and a radio, but I paid little attention to these conveniences, at least until 1938, when listening to the news took up much of my time.

The XX. District, in which we lived, formed with the II. District an island between the Danube River and the Danube Canal. We were close to the canal, and I spent many hours on stretches along its XX. District shore. Inasmuch as I had no brother or sister, I would often walk by myself, flanked by bushes and staring at the sky. At one time I looked up and said to myself: tomorrow I will be eight. I still like to take a walk every evening before a birthday for stock-taking.

It was during my early years that I encountered a problem that surfaces for almost everyone: We do not live forever. This cognition is not so simple for a schoolboy who has just started his life. I remember standing in the stone hallway, looking out a window into the courtyard where beggars sang for a groschen and where my mother beat the dust from our carpets. Momentarily I had the thought of jumping out. It was the only time I have had such a temptation. As a mature man I became convinced that in a manner of speaking we are trapped in our bodies, which will self-destruct eventually if not before. At that point I settled for continuity in lieu of eternity, allowing only a purpose *in* life, as distinct from a purpose *of* life, to serve as my last bastion.

Martin Luther said that if he did not have his God he would rather be a pig wallowing in dirt. The fact is that I have had no God. My father is at least partially responsible for this state of affairs. His idol was Baruch Spinoza, who taught that God in His extensions was everywhere, in every rock and every human being. Much later I came to the conclusion that such a proposition could easily be reduced to a tautology: one may as well say that one is one, two is two, or three is three. My father did not tell me that the Dutch Jews of the seventeenth century had clearly seen the implication of a philosophy in which God was so completely at one with the universe, and that they had promptly excommunicated Spinoza. I suspected, however, that in my father's case, beliefs or nonbeliefs had little to do with religion.

He dragged me to the synagogue in order that I might acquire an identity. He wanted me to know the biblical words in Hebrew. Inevitably it was there I became a rebel. Already I was contrary-minded, turning away from religion, which at first became irrelevant to me and then an allergy. Yet I was captivated by the arts of religion, particularly religious music, and not only Jewish music. To this day I listen enraptured to the liturgy of the Russian Orthodox church. There is something penetrating in the voice of a Russian basso profundo, something soaring in the Russian choir. I am ensnared by the great Italians, notably the fascist tenor Beniamino Gigli in the Verdi *Requiem*. A stranger in a record store once told me that he could not live without Vivaldi's setting of Psalm 109, the *Dixit*, and I nodded with full understanding. In Paris I had the supremely good fortune of hearing a live performance of Rossini's *Stabat Mater*, and when I first listened to a recording of the young Mozart's "Italianate" *Laudamus Dominum*, the melody was piercing. In a conversation with a highly intellectual monsignor, I asked why Beethoven's *Missa Solemnis* was not heard more often in churches. He replied that the music

37

was so powerful that the listener would be paying homage not to God but to Ludwig van Beethoven. And so it is with my homage when I enter the mosque of the Dome of the Rock, or when I gaze at Jusepe Ribera's painting *The Holy Agnes*, or when I read Genesis.

In the Austria of the 1930s it was impossible even for a Jewish child to be completely insulated from the pervasive Catholicism of the country. One of my teachers in public school, a Jew who had become a Catholic, led the class in the Lord's Prayer. Carefully he stated that the Jews need not participate, but since the prayer was so "beautiful," he invited them to recite it anyway. Nothing this man could have done would have created a greater aversion in me for all the words in the New Testament. More than a half-century passed before my interest in this document was aroused. To understand the actions of a priest, Bernhard Lichtenberg, who prayed for the Jews openly in the Berlin of 1941, and who was tried and convicted by a German court for his act, I reached for the Gospels and read them in one evening. That is when I appreciated their power.

A child is influenced not only by elders. One of my friends, Heinz Aschkenasi, who was a year older than I, imparted to me a great deal about his interests and hobbies, especially geography. I must have accommodated myself to him for several years, until he expanded into astronomy, but I still heard from him after his emigration to Tarija, in southern Bolivia, from where he sent me detailed letters about local flora and fauna. Whatever he said, the word *Geographie*, which he pronounced with gravity, remained in my consciousness.

In my childhood, both my mother and father constantly reminded me of my good fortunes. I was shielded from privation. Never did hunger or want cloud my days. I should have been unqualifiedly happy. Indeed I was, with my daily coffee, or on those momentous occasions when my mother and I boarded a train in the summer to leave for some destination, the farther the better. The linear experience of being on a train was my awakening to space. I needed a window not only to see what was outside but to estimate speed. I had to listen to the rhythmic sounds which one can no longer hear, now that the tracks are seamless. The train opened the world to me. In my pre-atheistic period I imagined that after the completion of a reasonably long life, I would continue to ride in these trains, invisibly, as a ghost or a soul, without having to purchase or reserve a seat. This magnetism of the railroad never deserted me. In my adulthood I kept it a secret, of course, thinking that it would be regarded as an element of infantilism, even though I already realized that this contrivance of the industrial revolution had had an immense psychological impact, notably in Germany and Austria. The traveler in a modern German train, which is mostly bereft of the all-important compartments, still receives a schedule marking the kilometers between halts, and the time of arrival at each of these stops, so that the speed may be calculated en route. In the United States, where passenger trains are relatively slow and are no longer an optimal mode of travel between many cities, I have had to transfer my loyalty to airports and aircraft.

My cognizance of trains has affected my work, and for a long time I was preoccupied with them in a research project. Specifically I was interested in the transport of Jews to their deaths. Germany relied on railways not only for moving supplies and troops, but also for the so-called Final Solution, which entailed the transfer of Jews from all parts of Europe to death camps or shooting sites. The railway apparatus was not only very large; its administrative procedures were almost incomprehensible. I went from archive to archive, pondering the special trains, the assembly of their rolling stock, their special schedules, and their financing. After I had just completed my study, Claude Lanzmann visited me in Vermont to discuss his idea of making a major film about the Jewish catastrophe. He showed me a railway document he had found and I seized it like an addict to explain the hieroglyphic contents to him. "This I must film," he said, and I repeated my analysis before his camera. Lanzmann also borrowed a train from the Polish government. A retired locomotive driver, who had hauled Jews to the death camp of Treblinka, took the controls one more time. The train encircles the film, emerging, as if from a tunnel, again and again, to mark the end of the Jewish people in Europe.

At the age of ten I was presented with a precious book. Although it was bought not for my pleasure but as a required text for the *Gymnasium* I was to attend, it mesmerized me immediately. The book was an atlas. A masterpiece of cartography, it was made for the eye, with maps so finely shaded that they highlighted the distinctions between major and minor rivers, deeper and more shallow waters, higher and lower mountains. Railroad tracks were always sketched in red, and cities were shown with circles and lettering denoting their size. Soon I leaped across the topographical features to the international frontiers. Here was something new: the political world, the world of power. Needless to say, Germany's and Austria's territorial losses in the First World War were indicated on several maps, and understandably Palestine was absorbed in an Arab desert. The omission of Palestine, however, was made up later when my school, the Chajes Realgymnasium, which was a Jewish institution, supplied us with a map on which we could locate every settlement in the Jewish homeland.

I never became a geographer. When I was about eleven I did try to make use of Latin, which we were forced to learn, to write a short text of geography in that language. I must have believed mistakenly that my work would be admired. A few years later I had forgotten all my Latin, along with my Hebrew, but the maps were imprinted in my mind for decades to come. In 1938 and 1939 my geographic expertise was actually appreciated by prospective Jewish emigrants who would ask me, "Raul, where is Barbados? Where is Trinidad?" Geography, however, became for me something more than an array of place names. I was beginning to think in spatial terms. When I studied international law I understood without need for explanations what "territory" meant in the context of that law, and when I delved into the German Reich, its occupied areas and satellite states, I saw it in a specific space, widening and extending its measures against the Jews.

That I did not explore geography as such more deeply is primarily a result of my shortcomings, particularly in mathematics; but to a certain extent I also attribute my stoppage of progress in the cartographic arts to my discovery of history. We had been introduced to the subject of chronology in our history classes, of course, but the recital of Holy Roman emperors had instead produced a nebulous impression of perpetuation. The Viennese instruction in history had for all practical purposes smothered any sense of change or even of progression. Then came a man who imparted to everyone a powerful demonstration of historical presence: Adolf Hitler. The impact of his appearance was unmistakable. In the hallway a Christian neighbor was crying because her thousand-year-old Austria had ceased to exist. The next day giant swastika flags were draped from the upper stories of apartment houses; photographs of Hitler were hung from windows; and marching youths with drums were moving through the streets. Jews, huddling in their apartments, breathed the ominous air and wondered what would happen to them if they did not emigrate in time. "Hitler will put us to the wall," my father said.

My childhood had ended in one stroke. I listened to all the conversations of the adults, and I was not excluded from their anxieties. I was riveted to the specter of unfolding events. Nothing escaped me now: the endless truck convoys filled with troops moving to the Czechoslovak border; Hitler's ultimatum that, come what may, he would march into the Sudetenland on October 1, 1938; the occupation of Prague; Japanese offensives in China; the Phalangist victory in the Spanish Civil War. As I gazed from the window, observing the scene, a thought fleeted through my mind: Some day I will write about what I see here.

On April 2, 1939, we were on a train moving slowly across the Rhine bridge linking Kehl, Germany, to Strasbourg, France. A German woman approached my mother in the corridor of the railway car and, full of curiosity, asked my mother for her reactions to the Nazi regime. She was a fashion expert on her way to Paris for a look at *haute couture*, the only field in which Germany still conceded superiority to the French. My mother replied that she would not speak until we had reached Strasbourg. A few minutes later we were free and—to be precise about our new status—refugees. In my mind this change, despite the advent of rootlessness and poverty, was completely positive. My parents still provided for me, and so far as I was concerned it was *they* who depended on my mother's family or occasionally on Jewish refugee relief agencies along the way. I was carefree. Not only had I escaped from Nazi Germany but I was expanding my acquaintance with the world exponentially. For a week we remained in Paris, waiting for a ship to Cuba that we would board in La Rochelle. Paris was a revelation to me. I noted that the poet Heinrich Heine had lived there. The Rhine in Düsseldorf, from where he came, is wider than the Seine, and he sometimes pined for the Altstadt—Düsseldorf's old core, where he was born and where he grew up—but he must have been drawn irresistibly to Paris, as I was. Paris, perhaps more than any city I know, had everything for everyone. One could not be lost there; one could only find oneself. I had occasion to test my reaction at intervals during later decades, and it never mattered what I did there. On my sixty-second birthday in 1988, I was still able to take an intoxicating walk through the throngs on the Champs Élysées.

My excitement in April 1939 was not dimmed when we

went on by train to La Rochelle. As we moved south I noticed the many soldiers, some of them Africans, at the sta-
tions, and permitted myself a conclusion that turned out to
be my first error of judgment in world affairs. If Germany
tried to attack France again, I thought, it would bleed to
death there.

The ship, the *Reina del Pacifico*, was English, and so was
its food. For most of the eleven-day voyage I was seasick,
but for a few days, as the vessel moved into the tropics, I
tried to walk on the deck reserved for third-class passengers.
There was a single small social room with a single phono-
graph and a single record that played the "Donkey Sere-
nade" over and over. Perhaps this music was an unsubtle
message of what the British management thought of the
passengers assembled there: Jewish refugees embarked for
Havana, Cuba; middle-class Chinese on their way to South
America from Canton, a city occupied a few months earlier
by the Japanese; and Cuban communists who had fought as
volunteers on the losing side in the Spanish Civil War, just
ended, and who were going home.

My Cuban interlude lasted a little more than four
months. I would not have minded a longer sojourn in Havana, for I felt alive there. We lived in a "hotel," in the old
part of the city, on the corner of Calle Habana and Calle
Muralla. It was filled with Jewish refugees and its rooms
were partitions, without a ceiling, capped only by a roof.
When someone turned on a light it illuminated the other
cubicles as well. The showers and washroom were at the
end of the hall, and each family had a table with chairs in the
corridor. The summer was hot and insects were everywhere,

from flying cucarachas to ordinary sugar ants. I remember a poor refugee who found ants inside her loaf of bread and exposed the cut bread to the sun in the hope the ants would leave.

My father and I walked a great deal in Havana, and I listened to the cacophony of musical sounds blaring from the open windows of street-level apartments. Some of the sidewalks were so narrow that a passing trolley would force pedestrians to press against the wall of a building. Everywhere there was loud conversation and shouting. The ubiquitous oranges, sold from carts, were cut in half and eaten by their buyers on the street. Coffee and milk were poured with both hands into the cup of a patron who would regulate the proper mix with continuous instructions. A chain of fifty Chinese restaurants, the Fonda, dotted the city and offered meals for a few cents. In an amphitheater police and army bands entertained the public free of charge. The concerts were always offered in two parts: the first half was classical, featuring such works as Wagner's *Tannhäuser* overture, which were applauded politely; but for the second half the instruments for the Cuban rumba and conga were added, and the audience became more animated until it went wild with the rhythmic playing of the dances.

In Cuba I also had my freedom. I do not mean the feeling of an adult who has just left a totalitarian country, but the elimination of the constrictions imposed by school. Most all our books were in storage, but I had three, including the atlas, which I always carried with me. The other two books were a novel, written by a German who had crossed the United States as a tramp on freight trains, and a volume

45

of plays by Shakespeare, in German, of course. I read both the novel and the plays for my amusement. Two tutorials were nevertheless imposed on me. My father himself took charge of my Hebrew, which he feared was slipping from my mind. He tried valiantly to have me memorize in the original as much of Genesis as possible. The brevity of Hebrew, he assured me, was one of the marvels of the world; the power of its sentences could not be duplicated in any other language he knew. The more of these sentences I could retain, the better a man I would be. I fully understood Genesis, and its literary impact on me was unmistakable. "You write short sentences," an editor once complained to me. I still do, though sometimes I hide this quirk with suitable connectives and, on rare occasions, semicolons. My Hebrew, however, was not to be salvaged. It went the way of Latin. The fact is that I started with the wrong languages. Many years later I read an article by a colleague about the fate of the Norwegian Jews. One of his footnotes puzzled me, and so I called the author for an explanation. He struggled with an answer, comparing his source with his note, and finally blurted out: "Raul, why don't you know an important language like Norwegian?" He was right, of course, and he might have added Latvian, or Lithuanian. . . .

I also had to learn a new language in Cuba, not Spanish—for soon I would have to leave this island—but English, which was to be my next vehicle of discourse. In Vienna I had already heard English in broadcasts of the BBC. I knew that in order to speak it I had to adjust my mouth, and I practiced these contortions in the mirror, also lisping as

46

one was supposed to. In the *Gymnasium* the instructor in English was practical. He did not burden us with grammar (I soon learned that there was none, at least by German, Latin, or Hebrew standards) but taught us "Pat a cake, pat a cake, baker's man." In Havana my tutor, thinking that Kipling's jungle stories were appropriate for my age, introduced me to that author. But when I came to the United States I could not tell someone the time.

The United States used annual quotas to regulate immigration. They were assigned on the basis of birth in a foreign country. My parents, born in a part of Austria-Hungary that was Polish between the two world wars, were admissible only under the relatively small Polish quota. Austria, where I was born, was considered for quota purposes to be a part of Germany, and therefore I was eligible to enter the United States under the much larger German quota. My father had registered himself, my mother, and me at the American consulate in Vienna on the same day, but for them the waiting period was ten months longer than for me.

After traveling by ship with a Cuban couple to Miami, where I arrived on September 1, 1939, I saw the tabloid headline WAR STARTS. Having heard that the American press would print anything to sell papers, I ignored them. For two days on my way to New York I did not think about Europe. On the bus, which had tiny windows, I caught a glimpse of America. The one sight that remains in my memory as we traversed the South was that of benches marked "For Colored." I reflected on the fact that I, who was not allowed to sit on a Viennese park bench stenciled *Nur für Arier* (For Aryans Only), had instantly been catapulted into a position above that of many Americans who had been born here.

On September 3 in New York I met several family members on my mother's side: the matriarchal aunt Adela and most of her children. The first cousins were considerably older than I. One of them, with whom I lived for the first two weeks, had a small daughter, the first of yet another generation. I was then shifted to Adela's apartment, where I joined her husband and her two adult unmarried children. Adela's daughter Gertrude, who played the violin, was the sort of person who could teach little children how to hold a bow and move it across the strings. I liked Gertrude immensely.

On my first day in New York I was naturally in the center of my family's attention, but the questions I was asked were interrupted as everyone gathered around the radio to listen to the British and French declarations of war on Germany. War had indeed begun, at least for the Poles, who were being overrun by German armies. For me this development was a signal to start a diary. Each day was allotted a line, and the only entries pertained to the progress of the war. In other words, I read the war communiqués and carefully noted invasions and the capture of cities.

In New York I was no longer spared from school. Only days after my arrival I was registered in the Abraham Lincoln High School, where I would spend the next three years. While one of my cousins and I were waiting in a small room for an interview and forms, I noticed an older man and his son who were there for the same purpose. The man walked up to me and asked me in German whether my name was Hilberg. He had never seen me before but had known my father in Vienna. His son Erich (later Eric) Marder became my lifelong friend. Both Eric and I lived three or four miles from school, and to save the cost of the trolley ride (five cents) we walked home together, discussing Jewish politics and the larger questions of life. In the fifty years or so since, we have largely dropped Jewish political issues, but we are still engaged in exploring selected existential questions.

Even in retrospect my overall impression of Abraham Lincoln High School is such that I must pause in the middle of the sentence to regain my composure. The atmosphere struck me as totalitarian. Student patrols were posted in the corridors. When I first received my program, I was supposed to report daily to a room with a three-digit number and an "L." Day after day I looked frantically for a number with an "L," but there was none. Finally I learned that the room was "prefect class," which met only for the purpose of checking attendance, and that the "L" stood for "late session." For several decades I relived this horror in my dreams. Gymnastics was an abomination, destroying every vestige of dignity and privacy a human being of any age should be entitled to in civilian life. "I don't like your rotten attitude," the gymnastics teacher told me. I did not have much to look forward to in my other classes, either. Science and mathematics were taught to elevate geniuses and brand the untalented. These subjects, as I should have known right away, would not be the bedrock of my career. The course in European history, on the other hand, taught by a woman who could not hide her communist sympathies, was laughable.

As I look for saving graces in this system, I can think of only three. One was a speech class for foreigners, in which accents were worked on. I now wish I had received more of this instruction. Another was the "creative writing" class, which was noteworthy not for what was taught there, namely next to nothing, but because it was an island of freedom. Finally I must mention a teacher in American history, Alfred Nussbaum, who pronounced the "u" in his name as in "us." Mr. Nussbaum was a follower of the now half-forgotten Charles Beard, who had emphasized the economic basis of history and politics. For me such an approach was much too confining, and I would probably have forgotten Mr. Nussbaum were it not for his manner and one particular incident, both of which were unusual.

Mr. Nussbaum was utterly convinced of the importance of what he was teaching, which is a fundamental prerequisite for any effective classroom presentation. "Can't you see," he would say with reference to some point that, if missed, would assuredly result in a permanent perceptual disability. One day I did not bring my homework, which he would inspect by walking through the rows at the beginning of the class hour. It was Monday, and the date was December 8, 1941. On the Sunday before, I had dropped all my usual activities, acutely aware that Japan's attack on the United States and Great Britain had opened a new chapter in history. When Mr. Nussbaum asked why I had not done my homework, I made no attempt to conceal my reaction to his question. "Because I am not a historian," I said sarcastically. "But you *are* a historian," he answered calmly. Some forty-five years later he came to a lecture I gave at the Graduate Center of the City University of New York, which hosted a small Holocaust conference. During an intermission I told the story of my December 8, 1941, exchange with Nussbaum to a colleague, Lucjan Dobroszycki. "Funny," said Dobroszycki, "Nussbaum just told me the same story."

Not very long ago the principal of the high school called me in Vermont to ask whether I would speak to the school. No, I said immediately, my schedule was already more than full, and I could not muster the time for a trip. In truth, I had never set foot there since my graduation, and I had always been convinced that virtually all the graduates of this institution kept their incarceration in the place a secret. But then a colleague who was in the biochemistry department of our medical school, and who, it turned out, was also an alumnus of the high school, shared with me a two-page newsletter that the principal had mailed to several of the alumni. Evidently some of them had accomplished something. One was the novelist Joseph Heller, who probably had the same creative writing teacher. In addition there were three Nobel laureates in the sciences.

I was a thirteen-year-old high school student in 1939 and a sixteen-year-old college student in 1942. The first two years in Brooklyn College were even more depressing than the preceding three in high school. I worked part-time in Manhattan factories, and at the insistence of my father, who strongly believed in the practical value of chemistry, I concentrated my major study in that discipline. My misery grew. When I had a seat in the subway I read irresponsibly, be it Hemingway or Tolstoy, Spengler or Nietzsche. Finally I became eighteen. The war was still on and the United States Army liberated me from chemistry.

Crossroads

WHEN I WAS STILL in basic training, an unusually perceptive sergeant told me that I could be a corporal or a colonel, but that I could not be a military man between these ranks. I was a poor soldier at the start, because I could not accept shibboleths like the senseless "general orders," which I refused to memorize. When the company commander decreed that I would not have the privilege of a pass to the city of Spartanburg, South Carolina, he found me quite content to stay in the camp on Sundays. I then obtained the pass as a punishment. When he asked me *why* I was the only man in the company who had not learned the general orders, I replied that evidently I could not master them. He became angry and actually considered sending me to officers' training school. I did not become an officer, but I was intensely interested in the war and was given the task of explaining it to the other trainees in the company.

Grand strategy was not my only interest. I began to wonder why the American infantry was equipped with the clip-fed Browning automatic rifle—with which an expert could fire single deliberate shots but which had 103 parts that could jam easily—while the German army had a light machine gun, which was a terror weapon with a high cyclic rate of fire and a barrel that could be changed in seconds when it became overheated. The American hand grenade seemed to me a tribute to the game of baseball, and I seriously considered the possibility that, beyond all the calculations involving the need to fight overseas and the attendant problems of supply, infantry arms could also be an expression of national character. The American, I believed, had a faster reaction time than his German opponent, and he sought ways of acting quickly in crisis situations, but for this reason he also dreaded and felt trapped in an artillery barrage, not armored by the psychological stamina and fatalism of his European adversary. Such were some of my thoughts during my first months in uniform.

From the moment I boarded a troopship to Europe, I became hyperalert. Everything within view and hearing I imprinted in my memory. I did not, however, have the searing experience that was the lot of millions of people in wars. I cannot compare my record with the long agony my father endured. I was not wounded and received no medals. Unlike so many American soldiers, I was not shelled at Anzio, did not cross the Rapido River, and did not wade ashore under withering fire on Omaha Beach. For years and decades I was told that I could not imagine what it was like. I heard this phrase over and over, not only from Americans but from a one-legged German veteran who had been trapped in the Demyansk pocket in 1941, and from survivors of Auschwitz. My brush with the war was very brief. Although I carried a rifle, I felt less than I observed.

I do remember a moment at two o'clock in the morning

when our troopship was rocked by explosions. Having always made distinctions between kinds of death, the watery one was especially threatening. Lying in my bunk, I imagined the waves rushing in and the ship going down with its thousands of soldiers trapped inside, a pandemonium and a drowning. The explosions, it turned out, were caused by our own depth charges to discourage what might have been an enemy submarine penetrating the cordon of warships in our convoy. On land I somehow felt more secure, even when I was awakened by explosions shaking the ground under me in a replacement depot. Was I the European in an American uniform?

One time I came away with an image rather than an experience. It was April 1945 in Bavaria. I looked at a field bathed in the sun. During the night the Germans had attempted to assault our lines. Our machine gunners had mowed them down. All over the field the bodies of the Germans lay motionless, rifles stuck in the ground to mark their location. One corpse was on its back, its eye sockets filled with blood. What, I asked myself, could have compelled these men at this late stage of the war to run into almost certain death? Was it the forlorn hope of being spared? I already knew that the state, and its political order, rests on the possibility of an ultimate resort to force by a government acting against its own citizenry. The men who, with barking officers behind their backs, made their suicide run were proof of the viability of this system. But why had they followed such an order? Why did they not mutiny?

I gathered impressions at a furious rate, but as a soldier I was, of course, a novice, and the war was over before I could be anything else. Our division stopped in Munich, and there we were quartered for several weeks in the former Nazi party headquarters. I had reached the center of the Nazi movement just after its demise, fingering the books of the Nazi party library, including a party edition of Martin Luther's treatise *About the Jews and Their Lies*. I mistrusted that publication until some years later when I read the original sixteenth-century book in the New York Public Library. In the party building I also spotted about sixty wooden cases. Still in possession of my skills as a shipping clerk, I opened a few and discovered that they contained Hitler's private library.

When I returned to the United States I was sent to intelligence school. Now I learned all manner of things that I should have known before I interrogated any German prisoners. My major course was "Order of Battle," the organization of foreign armies, a subject I recognized later as a proper subcategory of political science. For the first time I plunged into my studies with eagerness. It was during this assignment that I was promoted to technician fifth grade, the equivalent of a corporal. One of my classmates, a sergeant, Francis Winner, was one of the brightest men in the army. At the school we fought the war over, and in our competitive exercises I beat him only once, when I drew a situation map of the Battle of the Bulge. He had crowded his map too much, a familiar failing of American cartographers.

One weekend, Winner and I drove to his home, a pig farm in Iowa. It was an all-night drive, and so we had to have an agenda. He proposed his favorite topic: land mines, one of which he had sent home by parcel post from Germany for closer study. I countered with comparative machine guns. When our weapons discussion was exhausted, he came to the real point. He wanted to stay in the army. He wanted to be a cadet at West Point. He wanted to become a general. My immediate thought was, You can be a sergeant or a general, but what about all the intermediate ranks? Out loud I reminded him that he was over twenty and that he had been wounded on the Remagen Bridge. Furthermore he had another problem: Would there be another war? He wanted to be a major player and he understood, even in his sergeant's uniform, that a military man could not find fulfillment without a real test, a real contest. I lost track of him, but some forty years later I learned that he had become a major general in the reserve, dealing with legal matters. Had he reached his goal? And I, what was to become of me?

Returning to Brooklyn College, I jettisoned my chemistry. My remaining subjects of concentration were history and political science. In political science I found my intellectual home. I hungered for a structure, and soon I found two of them in the context of political science courses: government and law. Yet it was a historian at college who, more than any of his colleagues in the political science department, was to have a deep and lasting influence on me. His name was Hans Rosenberg. An expert in Prussian bureaucracy, he labeled his course "The Rise of the National State." He spoke in complete sentences and paragraphs, and each lecture was a chapter. In his presentations the bureaucracy became an organism. Its cells underwent amalgamation and interfusion as it took root in the territorial domain of the state, evolving and developing with a tenured meritocracy into an indispensable and indestructible system. As I listened to his lectures I began to identify "government" more and more with public administration, and I became aware of the concept of jurisdiction, that bedrock of the legal order, which appeared to be both the basis and the basic tool of the bureaucrats. These potentates were an unstoppable force. As administrators they would always follow precedent, but if need be they would break new ground, without calling attention to themselves or claiming a patent, trademark, or copyright. The bureaucracy was a hidden world, an overlooked world, and once I was conscious of it I would not be deterred from prying open its shuttered windows and bolted doors.

Like me, Rosenberg was a refugee from Germany, but from what I heard he had no connection with the Jewish community. His course covered the years from 1660 to 1930, a stopping point that at the time was customarily observed by historians who shied away from the present. Once, he overstepped his self-imposed limit and spoke of the German resistance movement during the Second World War. Another time he remarked, in parentheses, that the Napoleonic atrocities in Spain had not been equaled since. At this point I raised my hand and asked, "What do you call six million dead Jews?" Ah, said Rosenberg, that was an interesting problem, but one which was very complicated, and he was constrained by time and the outline of the course to forgo a discussion of my question. The whole incident took but a minute, and I believed that I was very calm. Many years later, however, a woman who had been in the class and who remembered the exchange exactly, said that I had been so tense that my fellow students were concerned about me.

Although I perceived in Rosenberg's remark about Napoleon a plain denial of Adolf Hitler's Germany, I used everything he taught. I did not even discard the word "complicated," with which he had answered me. To the contrary, the idea that the destruction of the Jews was complex became a fundamental hypothesis that guided my work. This complexity was to be uncovered, demonstrated, and explained. The killing, I became convinced, was no atrocity in the conventional sense. It was infinitely more, and that "more" was the work of a far-flung, sophisticated bureaucracy.

As yet, however, the inchoate thoughts swirling in my head had not reached tangible form. I had to entertain, however briefly, a choice dictated by the division of more advanced studies into law schools and graduate schools. You must go to law school, said one of my professors. You should earn law *and* graduate degrees, I was advised by a professor in graduate school, who held both. I could afford only one program, even with the help of veterans' benefits, so I became a student in the Department of Public Law and Government, as political science was called in the graduate faculties at Columbia University. I would concentrate on public international law, a field that soothed me and gave me peace. I mastered the logic of this law and spent long days reveling in such topics as state succession and reservations to multipartite treaties. Briefly I weighed the possibility of writing a dissertation about an aspect of war crimes, and then I woke up. It was the evidence that I

59

wanted. My subject would be the destruction of the European Jews.

As I thought about my plan concretely, I was able to enroll in classes of two highly knowledgeable men. One was Salo Baron, who had set himself the task of writing about the entire sweep of Jewish history, in twenty or more volumes if need be. His vision was more complete than that of any of his predecessors. It was to encompass all the domains of the Jewish experience: political, economic, social, and religious. Later I heard it said that he was in a trance, writing incessantly as he became older until he was enfeebled and died—his work still unfinished.

Baron would come to his class directly from his apartment nearby, take off his coat, sit down at his desk, and lecture without notes like a pianist embarking on a sonata. Moreover, Baron was not only the player but also the composer. He delivered his chords faultlessly, and I wrote down what he said as completely as I could. The yellowed pages are still in my possession—the only such folder I have saved from my student days—and when I decided to reread them after many years, I was amazed by the extent to which I had incorporated his thinking. It was a course in modern Jewish history, which Baron had divided into eras before and after emancipation, but in which he constantly stressed the independent life and separate fate of the Jews in all the lands of their residence. He spoke of the Spanish certificates of purity—*limpieza*—issued by the Inquisitorial courts of the fifteenth and sixteenth centuries and showing the Jewish descent of professing Christians, sometimes to one-sixteenth of their ancestry. He would point out that a book published by a Jew in Salonika would be read by his brethren in Amsterdam and Krakow, even while the Krakow Jews were ignorant of a Polish book published in their own city. Yet there was safety in this isolation, he said. When the emancipation was promulgated in several countries of Europe, it was not only uplifting but threatening. It was not an act of goodwill toward the Jews but a necessity of the national state. Jewish society responded nervously, he indicated, by making efforts to shift Jews into more "productive" pursuits, such as agriculture and manufacture.

I came away from Baron's course with an impression of Jewish apartness, of a long-lived self-contained community that had to cope with the new expectations of governments and that had become newly vulnerable as it emerged from the ghetto. Already I was thinking of Jewish defenselessness under the Nazi regime. When I asked Baron for bibliographical references to explore my subject, he asked me whether I wanted to write my doctoral dissertation under his direction. No, I said, I was a student of public law and government, and I was going to ask a professor in that department to be my guide. His name was Franz Neumann.

I had already decided to write about the German perpetrators. The destruction of the Jews was a German deed. It was implemented in German offices, in a German culture. I was convinced from the very beginning of my work that without an insight into the actions of the perpetrators, one could not grasp this history in its full dimensions. The perpetrator had the overview. He alone was the key. It was through his eyes that I had to view the happening, from its genesis to its culmination. That the perpetrator's perspective was the primary path to be followed became a doctrine for me, which I never abandoned.

Franz Neumann was to bring me closer to my goal. As a new visiting professor in 1948, he taught a course in German government which was packed by more than one hundred graduate students. He was forty-eight years old. Because he was hard of hearing, he would respond to questions with a bellowed "What? What?" His lectures were delivered in a staccato manner. His observations came like hammer blows, and conclusions sounded like announcements: "Germany became a democracy twice—both times by decisions of military authorities." Neumann began with the Middle Ages, holding his class in suspense until he reached the Nazi regime. That subject was his specialty, and he had explored it in an audacious book which he called *Behemoth*.

I read Neumann's work, which was one of our texts, from cover to cover several times. Its style, like that of the lectures, was dry, declarative, unadorned. The opening sentence of his concluding chapter begins with the words, "We have finished our discussion." But what a discussion and what a conclusion! With one decisive, sweeping motion he determined that Nazi Germany had no political theory, that it had no Marx, that it was not missionary in character, that unlike communist or democratic systems it sought no converts. In a single, startling generalization he pointed out that under National Socialism the whole of German society was organized into four solid, centralized groups, each operating under a leadership principle, and each with legislative, administrative, and judicial powers of its own. These four hierarchies were the civil service, the army, industry, and the party. Operating independently of one another, without a legislature specifying their prerogatives, they coordinated their efforts with agreements that, in class, he caustically referred to as "social contracts." Here then I found a Nazi Germany that in its roots was anarchic, an organized chaos, but with a freedom to march into completely uncharted areas of action.

When Neumann wrote his *Behemoth*, the war was still in progress. He did not have the benefit of using captured records. All his sources were library materials, such as legal gazettes or industry journals. My own intention, on the other hand, was to exploit the internal correspondence of the perpetrators, which was secret from the Allied powers and the general public during the war but which was being sifted in Nuremberg for introduction as evidence in the trials of war criminals. From a few printed samples of this collection I formed my first assumption: The destruction of the Jews was not centralized. All four of Neumann's hierarchies were involved in this operation. I called this bureaucratic aggregate the machinery of destruction. As I read on, I discovered my second hypothesis in an affidavit by Rudolf Kastner, a Jewish leader in Budapest who had observed the fate of the European Jewish communities before the Hungarian Jews were inundated in the catastrophe. In one sentence of his description of events he noted that "The plan of operation was almost identical in all countries: at first the Jews were marked, then separated, divested of all property, deported and gassed." It appeared, therefore, that the Jews were destroyed in a progression of steps and that everywhere the sequence was the same. Considering, however, that the machinery was not unified and that it did not follow a basic blueprint from the beginning, such patterned action was remarkable. The Germans did not know in 1933 what they were going to do in 1935 or 1938. The ultimate goal of annihilation, which in German correspondence was called the "Final Solution," was not even formulated until 1941. There was, however, a direction that was characterized by ever more intensive, more drastic anti-Jewish activities. Along this path, the logic of the development emerged, for the simple reason that earlier, more harmless measures were always the administrative prerequisites for later, more harmful ones. In short, the destruction of the Jews had an intrinsic, or latent, structure. I called this phenomenon the destruction process.

Kastner had given me an indication of this process, but I needed a more exact specification of the steps. I had to construct an outline, rigid and comprehensive enough to hold any document that I would find, so that even if there were thousands of notes, I would be able to file all of them precisely in the order in which I would use them in my narrative. At this point I was stymied, and I felt there was only one man who could help me: Eric Marder. A conceptualizer and problem solver unlike anyone I knew, he listened to me one evening at the Port Authority Terminal in New York, where he was about to take a bus home. With a sheet of paper he untangled the maze right then and there. Three of the steps were organic: the definition of the Jews, their concentration, and their annihilation. The Germans had to define the concept of "Jew" before they could move further against their target, and they had to isolate the Jews physically from their neighbors before they could proceed with the Final Solution. The economic measures against the Jewish community, which I could not easily place in the scheme without Eric's help, had another, secondary logic of their own. They too followed the basic steps in a precise order: dismissals from jobs and transfers or liquidations of Jewish enterprises after the definition; special taxes and wages up to forced labor after marking or ghettoization; confiscations of the Jewish "estate" after the killing.

One of my professors in international law, who was born in Moscow at the beginning of the century, asked me why the Jews could not have been simply killed with bricks and bats. The answer, of course, lies in the limited effects of a pogrom. As I discovered later, Adolf Hitler already understood this basic limitation in 1919 when he discounted temporary and relatively ineffectual outbursts in the streets and advocated rational measures that would lead to a final result.

I had become sure of myself, secure in my decision, certain that I would fill in the pieces of my jigsaw puzzle. It would take all my limited knowledge, all my limited talents, but precisely for this reason it was the right project for me. "Man," said Goethe, "may turn wherever he will, he may undertake whatever it may be, always he will return to that path which nature had marked out for him." As yet, however, I was not prepared to approach Franz Neumann with the full scope of my plan and to disclose my nature to him.

I was only a first-year graduate student. Neumann, who had many protégés and who granted only fifteen-minute interviews, did not know me at all. I broached the subject of a term paper. It would be titled "The Role of the German Civil Service in the Destruction of the Jews." He nodded and asked me whether I knew who Franz Schlegelberger was. At the time I did not know that ranking official of the German Justice Ministry. He sent me to the poorly lit fourteenth floor of the Butler Library, where mimeographed copies of the Nuremberg trial documents were kept. Later I said to him that the topic was too big for a term paper. Would he agree to sponsor it as a master's essay? He nodded again. After he had read my trial run of two hundred pages, he objected only to one passage in the conclusion. It was my statement that administratively the Germans had relied on the Jews to follow directives, that the Jews had cooperated in their own destruction. Neumann did not say that this finding was contradicted by any facts; he did not say that it was underresearched. He said, "This is too much to take—cut it out." I deleted the passage, silently determined to restore it to my larger work. Then I said to him that the civil service was only part of the story. I would have to add the military, industry, and the party. Neumann nodded for a third time. Would he, I asked, sponsor me for a doctoral dissertation entitled "The Destruction of the European Jews"? I was prepared to hand him a tightly constructed twenty-page outline. Neumann said yes, but he knew that at this moment I was separating myself from the mainstream of academic research to tread in territory that had been avoided by the academic world and the public alike. What he said to me in three words was, "It's your funeral."

III
The Gamble

Documents

FOR MANY YEARS after my decision to write the dissertation, I was alone. I do not mean that I was cut off from all contacts with colleagues and friends. In the course of my employment in various jobs I met with other people, and I was always in touch with Eric Marder. To all outward appearances I led at least a seminormal life.

Yet I was living in a closed world, one in which I was isolated with my documents and the story that evolved from them. Now and then I would share a discovery with a young fellow specialist in Nazi matters, Frederic S. Burin II, or with Eric, but on the whole I was engaged in a lone endeavor. In the prevailing atmosphere, which drew the attention of American Jews to Israel and the Arabs, and which directed the thinking of Americans as a whole to the cold war with the Soviet Union, my subject was relegated to the past. This was the time when those—like survivors—who were plagued by memories, were told to forget what had happened, and when the Nuremberg trials were conducted not so much to understand Germany's history as to conclude unfinished business in order that Germany might be reconstituted with a clean slate in the North Atlantic community of nations confronted with the threat of communism. Under these circumstances I was reluctant to mention my preoccupation in conversations with strangers.

In fact, I believed I was the only person who was trying to unearth and describe the German upheaval against the Jews. Fred Burin, who was fluent in French and who kept up with new books in the French language, called my attention to a book by Leon Poliakov. Titled *The Breviary of Hate* (later translated as *The Harvest of Hate*), it was a succinct summation of the Holocaust, albeit concentrated on the drastic phase of the process. I quickly looked at the footnotes—they were references mainly to the Nuremberg trial records. Whereas I was in the midst of looking at virtually all the nearly forty thousand prosecution documents, and a number of defense items as well, he had used relatively few. His thesis, expressed in the title, that the root of the process was hatred, seemed in my eyes to be an antiquated supposition. The bureaucrats, I already knew, were not "haters."

A few years after Poliakov's book appeared, another colleague mentioned that he had seen a British monograph on my topic. He did not remember the author, and he thought the title was something like "The End of the Question." Before I even found the book, whose author was Gerald Reitlinger and whose title was *The Final Solution*, I called Eric Marder. Here was the possibility of a personal crisis. If the work was based on the same sources, if my project had already been done, I would have to cease my efforts. After I read the book I was more at ease. Reitlinger had dug into documents more extensively than Poliakov, but he belittled—was this a British trait?—what had happened. He stressed that the destruction of the Jews was an "attempt" which had not entirely succeeded. After all, entire communities of Jews, especially in the West but also in the Balkans, had been left alive. He reduced some of the perpetrators to mere bunglers. One of them, a young man in a key position who expedited the deportation of Jews from France, he described as "puerile" and "ridiculous," a "pettyfogging lawyer of the least possible consequence." I could not endorse such an approach and saw no compelling reason to abandon my work. My coverage would be greater, and I would describe the deed, and those who had implemented it, in full.

By the spring of 1951, however, I had exhausted my savings. Neumann offered me a temporary job to escort a delegation of Germans in Washington. I said no. They were social democrats, he explained. Again I said no. Shortly thereafter he offered me another position, one which would unite me with my documents as a member of the newly formed War Documentation Project.

The project was housed in a building near the waterfront in Alexandria, Virginia, which had been converted from a torpedo tube factory into a federal records center. What I found inside was absolutely extraordinary. The United States government had gathered up captured German records of the Nazi era, shipped them across the ocean, and reassembled them in that building, where they filled 28,000 linear feet of shelf. Each piece of paper was in its original German folder and each folder, usually with other folders, was in a box, several inches wide, standing upright next to other boxes. It took but one glance at all these documents to realize that their contents could not be read by one individual in a lifetime.

The collection was sparse in industrial records or those of old established ministries; some of them had already been returned to the newly created Federal Republic of Germany. There was, however, much military material, including documents dealing with such topics as procurement, forced labor, and the military regime in occupied territories. I was a member of a team that consisted, on average, of eight people. We had been brought in to examine folders and to fill out cards about them for government clients, principally the air force, which wanted to know what the Germans had discovered about the Soviet Union during the Second World War. As I understood our mission, we were engaged in target research, not merely or even primarily physical targets but all the strengths and weaknesses of the USSR, including the morale of the Red Army and the civilian population. No objective, however, was clearly spelled out for us, and our aims remained murky.

The director of the project, Fritz T. Epstein, who had been chosen for his library experience and his knowledge of German and Russian, turned out to have limited analytical abilities. He was a prewar refugee who loved all Germans, and he took great care, because of his name, to explain that he was a practicing Lutheran. "He looks like a Jewish cattle dealer from Hesse," one of my older coworkers, who was a Jewish refugee, declared in a conversation with me, hissing as he spoke. Epstein's son Klaus became a well-known historian, who later gained notoriety for a derogatory review of William L. Shirer's *The Rise and Fall of the Third Reich*.

The Federal Republic of Germany mailed the review to many historians and political scientists in the United States, without explaining, of course, that the Epsteins might not be practicing Jews.

Our Epstein wished to establish contact with members of other projects in the building. One of the individuals he found in his explorations was Gustav Hilger, an official of the German Foreign Office during the Nazi regime, who had processed the reports of killings by Security Police for Foreign Minister Ribbentrop, and who had also been the conduit for plans to deport the Jews from northern Italy. Hilger was to address us, Epstein announced triumphantly. In that case, I would walk out, I replied. Epstein retreated and said nothing more about his German diplomat.

Hilger was not the only German recruit in our vicinity. There was also a German colonel who taught some American military officers in a room next to ours. One of my young colleagues, who was excited about intelligence work and national security, was tempted to look into the German personnel folder of the colonel, which was kept in our building. He showed me the record and asked me to explain the colonel's assignments on the eastern front. I could see immediately that our German neighbor had been the transport officer of the Eleventh Army at a time in 1941 when that unit lent the Security Police enough trucks to transport ten thousand Jews from the Crimean city of Simferopol to a shooting site. The Jews could then be killed quickly enough to allow the German army to enjoy Christmas without their presence. The colonel and I, however, had something in common. We would both stand in front of the locked gate before the records center was opened at eight o'clock in the morning. He said "Good morning" on one of these occasions, and I stared at him, not answering.

My eagerness at the gate had a profound reason. I had just begun to understand what a document really is. Here I could see that it is first of all an artifact, immediately recognizable as a relic. It is the original paper that once upon a time was handled by a bureaucrat and signed or initialed by him. More than that, the words on that paper constituted an *action*: the performance of a function. If the paper was an order, it signified the *entire* action of its originator.

Documents also store information. They are texts which contain a great deal of what we call history. A vast number of the documents in the federal records center had never been examined. Since the government did not know precisely what was in the folders, all of them were labeled confidential or secret. For me the pristine nature of this collection provoked suspense. What would I find there? Virtually all the work I performed for the government was automatically of benefit to me as well. The sheer disentanglement of German jurisdictions, such technical questions as to whether a military Ortskommandantur in some small city was a unit or a local office—all these problems would have to be addressed whether I was doing the government's work or my own. Moreover, the Jewish fate, as I learned quickly, was not isolated from the events that exploded all over the East. I had to know a great deal about the German occupation and its ramifications in order to grasp the setting and conditions in which the destruction process took place. Finally, however, I was interested in my subject specifically—the mention of Jews and the separate actions taken against them. I was looking especially for these passages, and I knew that the more I looked, the more of them I would find. When I was rewarded with a discovery, I experienced a sensation that is best known to my fellow page-turners. It is an excitement that still comes to me when I run a microfilm through a machine. I recall traveling with teams of specialists for the United States Holocaust Memorial Council to the Soviet Union and the German Democratic Republic just before their demise. As we sat in the cramped archives of these countries, Robert Wolfe, a veteran keeper of records, who once headed the Modern Military Branch of the United States Archives, remarked that looking at all these files, which had been locked behind the Iron Curtain for so long, was like being at the creation again.

I cannot help thinking of the isolated archivists in communist Eastern Europe who had held the other half of the story. The USSR had its sophisticated missiles and hydrogen bombs, but it kept its German records wherever they had been captured, in dozens of regional and local archives. Finding aids were often handwritten for the few researchers who were permitted to set foot there, and in one of these archives a Natasha with sixteen years of experience still did not know what was in her collection. The archives in Potsdam or Leipzig were different. Communist controlled but efficient, the German personnel knew everything. One of the clerks in Potsdam talked about a list of special trains as a "famous" register. It was, of course, famous to the other six clerks.

Often I have been asked whether in all the years of my research any of the material in the documents has ever made me ill. In the main I have been immune from such a reaction, but I do recall an exception. Early in my work I came across a wartime record of a court action brought by a Jew who had been denied his ration of pure coffee on the ground that he had received the coupon by mistake. *That* story made me slightly nauseated.

In the gathering of my sources I have always remained a brute-force man. My watchwords have been comprehensiveness and quantity. The more agencies whose materials I could examine, the better, and the more paper in the files, all the better. Because the destruction of the Jews was so decentralized, it required the participation of all those agencies that had the means to perform their share of the action at the moment when the need for their contribution arose. The spectrum of offices that were ultimately involved in the process is synonymous with the concept of German government or the whole of Germany's organized society. That is the reason I could not dispense with any agency collection, why nothing seemed too remote. I would sit in an archive in Lvov reading the correspondence of local German officials dealing with gardens and ornamental horticulture to discover that the greens were used as camouflage in the camps. I would learn that church records of births and marriages dating to the middle of the nineteenth century were essential in proving who was of Aryan descent and hence not a Jew. I found that a Berlin company that manufactured flags also produced bales of yellow Jewish stars. But I did not always recognize the importance of every single document, nor was I consistently successful in interpreting key pieces of paper. Such failures were galling to me.

Once, at the beginning of my research, I discarded a record because it seemed superfluous. Heinrich Himmler, as Reichsführer-SS und Chef der deutschen Polizei, had placed an announcement in a newspaper depriving the Jews of their drivers' licenses. I was still in Vienna when this edict was issued, and I distinctly recall that in the adult circle of our friends the measure occasioned some hilarity. No one in this group had a car. It was a young German researcher, Uwe Adam, who in the 1970s pursued this subject further and was led to a significant realization about the fundamental nature of the Nazi regime. Apparently there was a Jew with a driver's license who claimed that a mere announcement in a newspaper, as opposed to a promulgation in a legal gazette, was without effect. One might ask what importance a legal gazette had in a country so absolutist as Nazi Germany. The answer, of course, was that an order directed at a segment of the public had to be issued by the office that had jurisdiction in the regulation at hand. Himmler may have thought of himself as solely in charge of Jewish matters even before the war, but he had not been named to such a command post, and drivers' licenses, which were a traffic matter, were within the sphere of the Transport Ministry. A legal gazette was a means to assure that the proper authority was taking the action. If a particular measure touched the competence of two or more agencies, a prior agreement between them was necessary. That is why the *Reich Legal Gazette*, which was the most important of its kind, would sometimes publish a decree signed by several ministers, the top name being that of the man in charge, but the others signifying with their signatures a participation in the origination and enforcement of the measure. That is the step that Himmler had omitted, and that is why the courts had a serious problem. Finally the highest court ruled that if the Reichsführer-SS had placed an announcement in the newspapers without arousing the protest of the Highest Reich Authorities, as the ministries were called, then his measure was law. Here I had overlooked an important development in the Third Reich. I did not clearly see the creation of an engine for the taking of initiatives. Not only Himmler but any number of potentates began to rely on the silent assent of their fellow functionaries to take ever more drastic and unprecedented measures.

Inattention to the value of a document was bad enough. Misconstruing the content of a communication, especially one that I regarded as pivotal, was worse. The item in question was an order signed by Göring, the Number Two Nazi, to Reinhardt Heydrich, chief of the Security Police, on July 31, 1941. It is but three sentences long and charges Heydrich with organizing the Final Solution of the Jewish Question in Europe. I took this order to mean that Hitler himself had decided that day to annihilate the Jews, and that Göring was acting as his deputy. There was evidence of restlessness in the bureaucracy now that forced mass-emigration plans had collapsed. In Poland the Jews had already been concentrated in ghettos, and in areas wrested from the Soviet Union the Security Police and SS brigades had begun sporadic killing. The time for widening these measures had come, and Göring's authorization appeared to be evidence that the thought was now being translated into action. My reasoning was not altogether wrong—the time *had* come, and Hitler had not only signaled his intentions in preceding months, he had underscored them later. But *this* piece of paper was not one of his orders. My misunderstanding was already in print for some years when Uwe Adam published his obscure book to demolish the Göring letter thesis. If a written order had been issued, he reasoned, it would have been handed by Hitler to Himmler, not by Hitler's subordinate Göring to Himmler's subordinate Heydrich. As soon as I read this argument it convinced me. Now, however, a new question arose: How was one to account for Göring's letter?

The answer came to me one day when a politically conservative publisher in New York asked me to look at a memoir to determine whether it was authentic. The author displayed the consummate knowledge of an insider. Unquestionably I was reading a slightly edited version of Adolf Eichmann's recollections, which he had dictated in Argentina. In his account Eichmann disclosed that he himself had drafted the three sentences for Heydrich, who submitted the text to Göring for his signature. Heydrich was seeking an open-ended authorization, and because of his excellent relations with Göring he obtained it. Heydrich did not know what Hitler would decide—he wanted to be the official with power in his hands once a decision was made. Eichmann went on to say that one day he was called in by Heydrich who told him the grave news that Hitler had decided upon the physical annihilation of the European Jews.

The order had been given orally to Himmler who had passed it orally to Heydrich.

I read the three sentences again. They had been drafted in bureaucratic language. This was not Göring's prose. Uwe Adam had unlocked yet another important characteristic of the process. I had thought only of the decisive steps in the destruction; I had paid no attention to the fact that the decisions themselves were taken in steps. Nor had I appreciated that there was an evolution in the procedure of decision-making, that gradually laws gave way to decrees, and decrees to announcements, written orders, oral orders, and finally no orders. The functionary who sensed the purpose of the operation had come into his own.

Uwe Adam was a young man who died young. He was a researcher with deep insights, and he asked questions that others had failed to raise. At a meeting of a United States–German committee which dealt with intellectual and academic reactions to the Jewish catastrophe, I asked the German side to provide academic positions for just three young historians who were known to me as pioneers in the field: Hans-Heinrich Wilhelm, who dealt meticulously with mobile killings in the occupied Soviet Union; Götz Aly, who first pointed to the role of statisticians and economists in the process; and Uwe Adam. Nothing happened, of course, in response to my plea, and shortly thereafter Uwe Adam was gone.

An Art

M Y POSITION IN THE federal records center did not last long. At the beginning of 1952 Fritz Epstein began to talk to me in a fatherly fashion about my need to write my doctoral dissertation. His admonition was prompted by a number of his own concerns. He wanted to replace the existing crew in order to hire men who would be totally beholden to him. I was most certainly not one of his favorite researchers, inasmuch as I had expressed some doubt about his ability to maximize the exploitation of our documentary collections, and I had even shared my opinion with Professor Neumann and another Columbia University professor. Epstein must have been aware of my evaluation of him, and his conversation with me was an understandable act of self-preservation.

Leaving was not so simple for me. I could not be indifferent to money, and I did not wish to be jobless again. When I explored other opportunities in Washington, I quickly discovered a stumbling block. I could put on a uniform or I could join the newly created Central Intelligence Agency, which was an equal-opportunity employer, but other offices in my range of interest rejected me because I was foreign born. Like Gustav Hilger and the German colonel, I could be used for a special purpose, but I was not trusted in principle. Years later I would explain to my class in American Foreign Policy that under the law Henry Kissinger could not have been appointed to the ranks of the Foreign Service. He could only be a high official, a secretary of state.

At the same time I knew I had a deeper problem. During the first few months of my stay in Washington, I had utilized my evenings and weekends to full advantage in the Library of Congress. I still remember leaving the library when it closed and walking along magnificent avenues deserted in the night. After a while, however, the War Documentation Project occupied all my thoughts. Instead of simply filling out cards, I was concerned about its direction and accomplishments. I could not write any chapters with leftover thoughts in leftover time.

Reluctantly I returned to New York to take up residence in the small apartment of my parents, assuring them that I would be responsible for a third of the household costs, which I would pay as soon as I had the means. In the living room I set up a bridge table every morning. There I sat for the next three years. My mother would occasionally ask me with an insistent tone when I would be finished, and then my father, sighing, would ask me the same question.

My plan had no room for compromises. With my handwritten notes on three-hole paper in sixty folders piled in front of me, I would write chapter after chapter in pencil, again on three-hole paper. All the documents were arranged in the order in which I would consult them. I was restricted only in my use of material in the federal records center. My knowledge of the confidential folders sometimes insured me against making a mistake, or more often it enabled me to see a connection, which might otherwise have remained invisible, between facts gathered from other sources, but I was not allowed to cite these files directly. In 1955 I returned briefly to the records center to make notes about newly declassified items; I had to wait many more years for the remainder.

Meanwhile I worked daily. When I had completed a major passage I read it aloud to Eric Marder for his reactions. I would not show anything to Neumann before the entire manuscript was complete. It was for him that I was preparing the dissertation.

To portray the Holocaust, Claude Lanzmann once said to me, one has to create a work of art. To recreate this event, be it on film or in a book, one must be a consummate artist, for such recreation is an act of creation in and of itself. I already knew this fact on the day I embarked on my task.

The artist usurps the actuality, substituting a text for a reality that is fast fading. The words that are thus written take the place of the past; these words, rather than the events themselves, will be remembered. Were this transformation not a necessity, one could call it presumptuous, but it is unavoidable. What I say here is not limited to my subject. It is applicable to all historiography, to all descriptions of a happening. My subject, however, was mighty, as the novelist Bernard Malamud would have said, or a Tremendum, as the theologian Arthur Cohen would label it, and to

slip or fall in this effort would have been tantamount to failing tremendously.

No literature could serve me as an example. The destruction of the Jews was an unprecedented occurrence, a
primordial act that had not been imagined before it burst
forth. The Germans had no model for their deed, and I did
not have one for my narrative. Yet later I became aware that
I was appropriating, transcribing, arranging something. It
was not a work of literature but a body of music. While I sat
at my bridge table during rest periods in the evening, I
would listen to the radio, which in New York afforded an
abundant choice of recorded symphonies, concertos, quar-
tets, and sonatas. My childhood musical training was such
that I remembered almost nothing anymore. I could only
listen and gradually assimilate what I was hearing.

There are Mozarts and Beethovens in this world.
"Mozart wrote masterpieces when he was fifteen," said a
college psychologist who specialized in the problems of ado-
lescents, Peter Blos, after I had shown him a feeble effort of
mine at writing during the academic year 1942–1943, when
I was sixteen. It was the most devastating comment ever
made to me about my abilities, and I have not been able to
put it out of my mind, even after I learned more about Blos,
a not quite Aryan refugee who was a Protestant admirer of
Luther and the Reformation. Mozart would forever be out
of reach. He could not be emulated; he could not even be
copied. I am stunned, listening to his music, be it an early
composition like the *Divertimento in D* or a later, overpow-
ering organ fantasia. Everything he did seemed effortless. It
is as if his mind produced a series of explosions, in the

course of which his hand was driven to write the notes or to glide across the keys of his piano. This was a god whom the ancient Greeks, were they alive in his century, would have celebrated and worshiped with abandon.

Not so Beethoven. *He* had to work, to build his music like an edifice, draft after draft, slowly, painfully. Four opening notes in his Fifth Symphony—I listened only to his odd-numbered ones—followed by four more, and thus he laid down his building blocks. I imagined him with four measures like these creating a phrase, and with this phrase a theme, and upon the theme the variations. But what architecture this structure became! The chords—those tones played simultaneously—were varied in turn. Not for naught is Beethoven called a master. All was controlled, taut to the ultimate degree.

I had to control my work, to dominate it as Beethoven had fashioned his music. Writing, like music, is linear, but there are no chords or harmonies in literature. For this reason I concentrated more and more on chamber music, which is sparse, and in which I could hear every instrument and every note distinctly. The Schubert Quintet in C—a Germanic work—gave me the insight that power is not dependent on simple mass or even loudness, but on escalations and contrasts. Beethoven's *Appassionata*, that supreme achievement of piano music, which proves that one keyboard can be the equivalent of an orchestra, showed me that I could not shout on a thousand pages, that I had to suppress sonority and reverberations, and that I could loosen my grip only selectively, very selectively.

I grasped for an overall symmetry. Beethoven, I learned

in a book by the musicologist Lewis Lockwood published in 1992, had sketched the finale of his *Eroica* symphony by pairing what he placed first with what he put down last, and then what followed the first with what preceded the last, and so on in candelabra fashion toward the middle. I had done something very similar with my twelve-chapter work. The first chapter was thematically reflected in the last. The second was matched with the next to the last, and the third with the tenth. The longest of my chapters was the one on deportations. It was the *andante* of my composition, with a theme and multiple variations that mirrored the special conditions under which deportations were carried out in each country.

The specific content of my text was given to me, of course, primarily by the records that the Germans had left behind, but there was a problem of rendition. Because these documents were in German, I could not embed them in my story without reproducing their substance in English. Languages are not the same. There are agglutinative words in German, as well as a great deal of heaviness, redundancy, and exclamation. One would think I did not have this difficulty when my books were later translated *into* German. But the German of the Nazi era is different from the German that emerged after the war. Extreme positions, and the absolute certainty with which they were stated in Nazi times, have been attenuated. Pristine German words have given way to a mélange of foreign and imported expressions. I was not fully aware of the extent of these changes until I received the drafts of the German translators. No, I would say, you cannot do that, a *Beamter* is not a *Manager*, a

Niederschrift is not a *Protokoll, misshandelt* does not mean *malträtiert*. You are losing the original style and feeling. You are ignoring the fact that every German sentence that one finds in a document of the early 1940s incorporated the whole culture and atmosphere of that time. You are actually translating one kind of German into another German. In my quandary I thought I might produce document books, but even if I were to do so in the original German, this exercise would be a compromise. Documents never stand alone. As fragments they should be interpreted and explained. If they are to become ingredients of a coherent account, they must first be selected, excerpted, and ordered. All of these manipulations are a way of imposing a meaning on the pure texts for the sake of intelligibility. In short, whatever the genre, I would still have the task of synthesizing my work in a manner that would retain, to the maximum extent possible, the thoughts of all those who created this history.

My training in the social sciences took place in the 1940s. The methodological literature that I read emphasized objectivity and neutral or value-free words. I was an observer, and it was most important to me that I write accordingly. At one time I said to Eric Marder that when, if ever, my manuscript appeared as a book, nothing should be said on the dust jacket about the personal experiences of the author. Needless to say, no publisher allowed me such anonymity, but the printed pages at least would be devoted to the subject, not the person who wrote them. To this end I banished accusatory terms like "murder," as well as such exculpatory words as "executions," which made the victims into delinquents, or "extermination," which likened them to vermin. I added charts and numbers, which added an air of cool detachment to my writing. I did yield to some temptations. Herman Wouk said to me that the work contained a suppressed irony, in other words, an irony recognizably suppressed. I also wanted capsule lines at the end of passages and chapters. I really weighed this decision, listening to Beethoven's extended finales but also to a violin concerto by Prokofiev that seemed to end in midair. In my resolution of this particular predicament I leaned toward Beethoven.

Above all, I was committed to compression. I had to avoid elaborations, detours, and repetitions, not only because they would diminish an effect but for the simple reason that I had to watch the size of my work. My estimates of length had been wrong. I needed more space and more time than I had thought. The task demanded comprehensiveness and it required balance: if this, then that. Brevity did not mean omissions, and the pages were piling up. I never regretted my tenacity in this regard. Claude Lanzmann did not miniaturize the event in his nine-hour film, and Herman Wouk did not do so in his two-volume novel. When I participated in the planning of the United States Holocaust Memorial Museum, I expressed the hope that it would not be small, and when the building was opened its sheer size was large enough to make a statement. Eric Marder approved of what I was doing. He suggested, half-jokingly, that I should hand my completed manuscript to Professor Neumann with the words: Here is my funeral.

By the fall of 1954 I could allow myself an encompassing glance at my work. Most of the pages were down on paper.

Even though I was teaching, I was still advancing toward my goal. I was in Puerto Rico then, and delayed news reached me that Franz Neumann had died in an automobile crash in Switzerland. Momentarily I broke down. Neumann had been important to me to a far greater extent than I had acknowledged. He was not only the political scientist who in his *Behemoth* had given me an indispensable tool of analysis, and he was not merely a professor on whom I was going to rely for the furtherance of my career. He was a presence that sustained me.

For the first time I reflected on *his* life. I had learned so little about him. Some of the details of his youth and family had surfaced in time, and so had the bare facts of his career, but I could not muster much more. I knew that he was a Jew who was born in Silesia and educated in Frankfurt, where he obtained a law degree; that he practiced labor law in Germany before moving to England; and that he studied under Harold Laski in London, where he earned a doctorate in political science before moving on to the United States. In 1942 he joined the Office of Strategic Services and later the Department of State, two agencies which employed refugees to decipher Nazi Germany. During his last seven years, in the Department of Public Law and Government at Columbia University, he was a phenomenal success. I heard that at the time of his death he was the sponsor of some twenty-six doctoral students. He had also published articles, which were quoted reverently, about such subjects as power and anxiety. To me they did not matter. What, after all, can a man do after he has written *Behemoth*? But this is a question that preoccupies me now and that I would not have asked aloud while he was alive or for as long as he might have lived. All I would have said then is that *Behemoth* would remain as the milestone that it was, and that I would henceforth be an academic orphan.

I V
On Struggling

Securing a
Teaching Position

FOR THIRTY-SEVEN YEARS I was engaged in teaching. A professor in my field will stand in front of a class and essentially tell a story two or three times a week over a span of approximately four months. The telling is supposed to flow, and that is why the lectures are called a "course." I taught one particular course, in basic international relations, at least sixty times.

My portfolio of offerings, especially during my first decade as a faculty member, was quite large. It included my first love, international law, and my primary offering, American foreign policy, but also world politics, geographic backgrounds to politics, American government, public administration, defense policy, and even methodological considerations in political science. All these courses were a part of the usual curriculum, and a new entrant in the profession had to be flexible. Fortunately I was an eclectic practitioner in my discipline. I actually felt a psychological need to investigate political institutions that were centered on everyday life. These laws, agencies, and policies were a wall of stability on which I could lean. Only later, much later, did I teach a course labeled "The Holocaust."

Obtaining a teaching position was far from easy. I battled three obstacles. The first, which affected all applicants, was the teaching market: Whereas many war veterans had been encouraged by available government benefits to pursue graduate studies, thus swelling the supply of men who were academically qualified to teach in colleges, the enrollment in classes was beginning to thin out, because the pool of potential students had to be drawn from the shrunken generation born during the economic depression of the 1930s. A second problem was discrimination against Jews, particularly in private colleges. The third was, of course, the peculiar subject of my doctoral dissertation.

I remember my first appointment, which consisted of teaching a night course in a business school training secretaries and sales people for service in Latin America. In February 1954 I obtained a lectureship at Hunter College in New York to teach four sections of American Government for four-fifths of $320 a month. Hunter College was one of the four colleges operated by the city of New York. In an effort by the city to promote a cultural "melting pot," it was the custom to install a Jewish president in Queens College, which had a predominantly Protestant student body, and a Protestant president in Brooklyn College, which was overwhelmingly Jewish. Hunter College, which was already a melting pot of students, albeit with few Protestants, had a Catholic president, George N. Shuster. I promptly looked up his qualifications and discovered that he had been a professor of German as well as a publicist who had written books about Nazi Germany before the war. In two of these publications he had also mentioned Jews, with references to the "fishmongers" of Krakow and the aesthetic appeal of the "daughters of Sarah." The Department of Political Science at Hunter College had three full professors, one Protestant, one Catholic, and one Jewish, all them women who looked somewhat elderly to me. Their sex and age may be explained by the fact that Hunter College had been a school only for female students before the war. I was handed a detailed syllabus, prepared by the Catholic professor, with which I was expected to teach. It emphasized the Constitution of the United States.

I loved the Constitution and could recite many of its provisions from memory. Had I been a member of the Supreme Court I would surely have slept with a copy of this document under my pillow, lest I awake in the middle of the night worrying about the wording of a particular clause without having the text immediately at hand. As a lecturer, however, I also wanted to teach something about the actuality of American government, and I wanted to be very broad in my presentation of its institutions. In this respect I was only following the greatest political scientist in America, Lord James Bryce, whose two-volume textbook, *The American Commonwealth*, first published in 1888, did not fail to include all kinds of bodies, among them universities. Having thrown the syllabus away, I obtained colored chalk and drew organization charts, discussing such ingredients of our commonwealth as the Defense Department, the independent regulatory commissions, and the educational establishment. The Jewish full professor, walking into one of my classes

95

unannounced to observe my teaching, could immediately spot my heresies on the blackboard. Later in the semester I wanted to say something about prejudice and discrimination, giving as a prize example the writings of the college president, George N. Shuster. When I discussed my plan with Eric Marder, he counseled against a public showing of this particular illustration in my class, basing himself on the supposition that I wanted to keep my job. I followed his advice, but now I wish that this one time I had not consulted him.

In the summer of 1954 an acquaintance working in the office of the president of the City Council called me. We had been employed for six weeks in a local Republican election campaign in 1949, and now, a Democrat, he offered me a modest position with a salary ordinarily payable to a typist. I thanked him, explaining that I already had employment at Hunter College. In that connection I told him about a letter that the chair (the Protestant woman) had sent me, thanking me for the work I had done and wishing me a pleasant summer as well as a successful next year. In other words, he said, I had been fired. For a moment I was dumbfounded. Could I have been so naive? He picked up the telephone right then and there and made me ask for a clarification at the college. He was right. I was unemployed.

I was dispirited by the prospect of working full time in a municipal office, so far removed from the national and international scenes, even though I was impressed with the fact that New York City had the second-largest public budget in the United States. Going to the placement bureau of Columbia University I asked if there was another teaching position. Did I have any geographic restrictions? I was asked. No, I replied, I would go any place where the American flag flew. In that case, I was told, I could take advantage of an immediate opening in Mayaguez, Puerto Rico, a city on the west coast of an island wrested from Spanish control fifty-six years earlier.

The position was in every sense an impossible assignment. The recruiter was William Hunter Beckwith, director of general studies at the Mayaguez campus of the University of Puerto Rico. We talked only on the telephone, because his time in New York was exhausted and he had to return to Mayaguez right away. He was interested in me, even though—or precisely because—I was unable to lecture in the Spanish language. Puerto Rico was United States territory, and it was important, he said, that college students there learn their subjects in English. After I arrived, I found that I was the only one *not* teaching in Spanish. Many of my students would nod in my classes, but not many understood what I was saying. Moreover, the course I was teaching was an introduction to the social sciences, with a syllabus synthesized by social science faculty members. It was clear to me that even if I spent all my time mastering the rudimentary elements of the subjects in which I was untrained, I could not do justice to the course outline. To be sure, the vast majority of my students were underprepared as well. The university stuffed itself with young people for whom there were no employment opportunities on the island, and in 1954 it accepted without much question Puerto Rican veterans of the Korean War, for whom the United States government paid tuition and monthly support.

97

The Puerto Ricans, unlike the Cubans, had never re-
volted against anyone. They were a most peaceful people,
with a touch of sadness. Even their national anthem, the
Borinquen, struck me as sad. In 1954 Puerto Rico looked like
an American colony. A minority political party, the Inde-
pendendistas, were striving to establish a republic. Another
small group, the Estadistas, wanted to be like Massachusetts
or Texas, with senators and representatives in the Congress.
Most Puerto Ricans, however, saw viability only in the status quo, as a relatively tax-free, low-wage island which could
attract American manufacturing enterprises to Puerto Rican
cities and export its own surplus population by the plane-
load to New York.

Yet Puerto Rico affected me in ways I had not foreseen.
My Puerto Rican colleagues accepted me unreservedly as I
was, without saying "if only" I would do this or that, without wanting to remold me in any way. I would listen to the
popular music, especially the *merengue*, but also to the
stately *danza*, which was old music of Spain, preserved on
the island by the Figueroa string quartet. In December
1954 I was invited to a Christmas party. The centerpiece
was a puny, possibly plastic Christmas tree, and everyone
sang the *Arbuelito*. It was almost as if I were in a trance.

I could not remain there. After Franz Neumann's death
all my expectations had become precarious. My only certainty was my resolve not to write another doctoral dissertation. I offered the first 22 percent of my manuscript as a
fragment for my degree, and approached Professor William
T. R. Fox to be my sponsor. Once, he had asked me whether
I wanted to write about the German satellite states—his

wife, Annette Baker Fox, also a political scientist, was interested in small countries—and I had declined. Although he had every right to turn me down in turn, he agreed in a magnificent gesture of magnanimity to my plan. By January 1955 I had my degree. By March of that year I learned that I had no job.

William Hunter Beckwith had sent a letter to six members of his faculty, asking for their resignations. He had not written six letters but one to all of the recipients. My notice was a carbon copy. I knew little about Beckwith. A middle-aged bachelor who had been a dean at Hofstra College on Long Island, and who reputedly had a substantial financial interest in a Brooklyn shipyard, he was a man of multiple talents. He knew Spanish and other languages, had been a missionary in the Philippines, and played Mozart on the piano as well, perhaps, as Albert Schweitzer played Bach on the organ. Some of my colleagues who had been imported from the mainland assured me that Beckwith was an outspoken bigot. One day they came to the restaurant, Johnny's Bar, where I had my supper every day, and asked me to lead a revolt to oust him. To an instructor in English, the folklorist Billie Wallingford Boothe from West Virginia, Beckwith had said trustingly that the Puerto Ricans were worse than the New York Jews. I agreed to be the leader. With the quiet support of the Catholic church and a key member of the Independendista party, we prepared our case. On April 26, 1955, we read our sixty-one-page statement aloud before a packed audience. We won and I returned, unemployed, to New York.

At the age of twenty-nine, my calculated debt to my father and mother was almost as much as I could hope to earn after taxes in a year. My only income in the fall was provided by an institute which sent me for a few weeks to Washington to survey the newly declassified documents in the federal records center. I salvaged these materials also for my own use, copying them frantically by hand. Then the winter came.

In January I received a call from William T. R. Fox. The University of Vermont had a temporary opening which had been created by the absence of two faculty members on consecutive leaves, and which was good for a year and a half. I told him that discrimination against Jews was widespread and that I probably would not even survive an interview. He tried to reassure me, saying that a state university was not allowed to discriminate. When I arrived in Burlington, Vermont, I learned that I was safe. The discrimination was directed at Catholics. Counting me, the nine-man Department of Political Science consisted of six Protestants and three Jews. An east-west street in this city of fewer than forty thousand people divided the Protestant and Catholic communities. Twenty years earlier, Catholics had not even been able to obtain employment as bank tellers.

During my interview I was not fully aware of these divisions, nor did I soon become acquainted with all the compartmentalizations within the university. Half the students came not from Vermont but from other states, and there was a considerable difference in the economic circumstances and career orientations between the two groups. Many of the out-of-staters, whose parents could pay the high tuition, were self-segregated in fraternities and sororities. Jewish students, most of whom also came from other states, had their own two fraternities and a sorority. In the women's dormitories, students were assigned to rooms by religion, wealth, and physical height. The social life of the students was closely monitored by the administration, lest there be inappropriate associations across religious or social boundaries, and the handful of young unmarried faculty were adrift.

The university had only about three thousand students, and when I was shown the library, a turn-of-the-century building with much interior wood, I asked where the principal collections of books were kept, only to be told that I was looking at them. From the dean I gained the impression that my research was my own private business and that I would be paid for my teaching. The pay, incidentally, was a thousand dollars less than my salary in the War Documentation Project four years earlier. All these drawbacks and limitations notwithstanding, I accepted the position unhesitatingly. Bolstering my morale, Eric Marder pointed to several positive elements in my new situation: I was going to be an assistant professor before I had reached my thirtieth birthday, and the university was instantly recognizable because it was named after a state.

After I returned to Vermont with my two suitcases a few days after the interview, I was told that my tight three-day teaching schedule had been changed to six mornings and five afternoons of classes. Instead of international relations I would be offering American government, and in addition to teaching my four sections of three different subjects, I would be participating in a seminar called "Popular Government." From the first day I decided that, no matter how heavy my load, I would never neglect my lectures. I plunged into the classroom with all my mental resources, relegating the completion of the remaining chapters of my book to my abbreviated weekends and typing finished pages before breakfast. At the same time I suppressed the thought that, given my rate of progress, the manuscript would not be finished for years.

One night I looked at myself as I was, and had insomnia. It was the evening of June 1, 1956. The next day I would be thirty. I stared at the ceiling from the ultrasoft mattress in the furnished apartment I had rented. A curtain separated the "bedroom" from the kitchen, where I had never cooked anything. I had rented this place in the middle of the Catholic French-speaking section of town as a gesture of protest, after a faculty wife had warned me that I was looking for accommodations in the "wrong" area of town. I walked from here to the office every morning, stopping for coffee on the way. Now I reflected on the fact that I had met only my departmental colleagues and that I had no private life whatever. What had happened to me?

In the summer I resolved to move out of the French section to rent a more spacious one-bedroom apartment near the university. Were it not for my furnishings, one might have concluded that I had already joined the middle class. They consisted of a plain bed with a five-dollar night table, an inexpensive sofa and chair, bricks and boards for my very small collection of books, and a dining table with a single leftover matching chair, which I acquired at a greatly reduced price, and which I used for my work. No curtains, no rugs, no television set, and no telephone. Also, no car. When I first set foot in the United States I had admired cars, often stopping to gaze at them in the streets of Brooklyn. Now I still could not afford one, and with the passage of time my hunger for a vehicle passed as well.

My employment was stabilized during the spring of 1957 with a change in my position in the university. Owing to the increasing popularity of political science among the students, the departmental teaching staff was to be increased by one person. Since I was already on board, I could remain. The alternative would have been yet another temporary position in a college situated in central Ohio.

An additional change in my fortunes was a grant, financed by a Jewish organization that received German reparations funds for the support of needy victims who were pursuing research projects in the realm of Jewish cultural reconstruction. Since I was considered a victim by virtue of my status as a refugee, and inasmuch as I was needy enough on the basis of my salary, I met two of the verifiable criteria for eligibility. As to my contribution to the enhancement of Jewish culture, I am not sure about the thoughts of the grantors. The title of my project, at any rate, clearly indicated that I was dealing with something that had happened to the Jews. I received $1,500—almost enough to repay all the remaining debt to my parents.

Although I had finally gained a steady position with financial freedom, I did not augment my living standard to any appreciable extent. One of the reasons for this forbearance was my continuing rootlessness. "Vermont is a disaster," my father said at one time. He did not see me walk in the icy wind to eat my supper in a cafeteria, but he sensed what my life was like. Although I had feigned happiness, talking about my friendships with younger departmental colleagues, especially the erudite L. Jay Gould, who grew up in Puerto Rico and who would call me *hijo* (son) while he listened patiently to all my troubles, my father knew that years after my arrival in that state I could have left it instantly with my two suitcases and a couple of boxes containing my books. I should note, however, that my social isolation was not the only cause of my restraint as a consumer. The additional consideration was a very specific worry. I had to ask myself how much money I might need to finance the publication of my book.

The Road to Publication

IN NOVEMBER 1955, before my appointment in Vermont, I was notified by the dean of the graduate faculties of Columbia University that I was the recipient of a Clark F. Ansley Award. This honor was conferred by the university once a year on two persons, one who had submitted a doctoral dissertation in a department of the social sciences, the other in a department of the humanities. That year more than seventy degrees had been granted in the social sciences alone. My dissertation was selected in a two-step competition. First I had been nominated by the Department of Public Law and Government, and then I won a contest with the nominees of the other social science departments. The prize consisted of a contract offered by Columbia University Press for publication of the chosen dissertation.

A door had been opened for me: I could look forward to seeing my work in print. I felt not only uplifted by this development but also grateful, particularly to William Fox, who had already rescued me after Neumann's death, sheltering me under his protective umbrella. When I told him later that I could not repay him, he said only that I should help others who might need me, and this I have tried to do, to the extent possible, from my base in Vermont.

Soon, however, a potential problem surfaced in a letter written to me by the publication manager of Columbia University Press, Henry H. Wiggins. The dissertation, for which the prize had been awarded, was not the complete manuscript. Would I, he asked in his letter of December 30, 1955, absolutely refuse publication of this fragment, if the faculty and the Press were to agree that "that and that only" should be published as the Ansley Award winner, and that publication of "more" of the work would have to be the subject of "separate and later" negotiations between the Press and me? I was disturbed by this guarded attitude, by the negative implication in his question, by the hint that a line could be drawn. I could imagine him drafting a memorandum to the faculty urging that in the future Ansley awards not be given to candidates whose dissertations exceeded a certain length.

My correspondence with Mr. Wiggins went on for three and a half years. In 1956 he revealed to me, in stages, the position of the Press. First of all, the financial responsibility of the Press was definitely limited to the dissertation portion. A subsidy would have to be obtained from a foundation for the remainder of the manuscript. Then he mentioned a reader. "Technically" the complete work would not be accepted by the Press for publication until a favorable verdict had been received from a designated referee.

I filed these letters while I was trying to complete my labor. What I had drafted before coming to Vermont I could edit and type with deliberate speed. All but the last two chapters were finished in 1956, but these concluding passages, which dealt mainly with consequences and implications in the postwar era, became an albatross with which I struggled until the spring of 1958. During that time I added not only pages to my manuscript but also dollars to my savings account. The sums were much too small to guarantee the publication of my work, but I stockpiled the money for the contingency that all else would fail and that I would have to provide a subsidy myself.

In October 1956 a complete stranger became interested in my manuscript. His name was Frank C. Petschek. He lived in New York and was a refugee from Czechoslovakia, where his family had owned coal mines. In an early chapter that was part of my dissertation, I had described the Aryanization of the Petschek properties, that is to say their forcible passing into German hands. "We have never had anything to do with banks," Mr. Petschek said at one time. When I looked at him questioningly, he explained that the Petscheks had never *owned* any banks.

Mr. Petschek's curiosity was aroused by a conversation reported to him by his daughter, who was a graduate student in political science at Harvard University. She had talked to one of her professors, Carl Friedrich, who had been one of the judges for an award presented by the American Political Science Association to the writer of the best political science dissertation of the year. I had been edged out for this award by Judith Sklar, a political theorist who had obtained her doctorate at Harvard for a study of "Utopia," but Friedrich was impressed with what I had written. He could not remember my name or the title of my dissertation, but he was certain that I had done my work at Columbia University and that I must have interviewed the Petschek family. Frank Petschek remembered no such interview and wondered how I had covered the story. Looking under "coal mines," "industry," and "German economy," in the Columbia University library, he could not find my dissertation. Finally he was handed my manuscript titled "Prologue to Annihilation." In the footnote references to the Petschek enterprises he could see citations of Nuremberg trial documents drawn from the files of German industrialists, bankers, and the Finance Ministry.

The library did not permit removal of a manuscript from the premises, and Mr. Petschek wished to read my account at home. He wrote to me for a copy, but those were the days when duplicate pages were made with carbon paper. The clear ribbon copy that I had typed myself was in the hands of the Press, and I asked Mr. Wiggins to lend it to Mr. Petschek.

By April 1957 Frank Petschek had read all of the sixteen hundred typewritten pages I had finished by that time. He asked casually whether the publication of the work was financially covered, and I replied that funds for the expected deficit had not been secured. Later that summer he told Wiggins that he was not the man who could provide the needed subsidy. Wiggins took that statement to be final. Why then had Mr. Petschek read all those chapters that dealt with the Final Solution? He was a Jew. His wife's family had been killed. In addition, he had a sense of responsibility, undoubtedly derived from the fact that he had once

been a major businessman. He wanted to see this manuscript become a book; he did not want to drop it or me. At
the same time he was acutely aware of how much his resources had shrunk. His small foundation supplied colleges
with slides of his favorite Dutch landscape paintings. He
had shown me a copy of a world almanac in which he had
put check marks next to some of these needy colleges.
Clearly Mr. Wiggins wanted more than slides.

Another interested person was Philip Friedman. When I
defended my dissertation in January 1955, he was on the examining committee, where he had replaced Salo Baron.
Friedman was not a philanthropist but a survivor, margin-
ally employed as a lecturer in history by the university. He
was interested in the Jewish scene in Poland and hoped to
write a book about ghettos. It did not come to that because
he died early, before undertaking the project. He did read
my dissertation with care, and he had various connections
with institutes. Since he lived in the Jewish world, he recommended joint publication of the complete work by Columbia University Press and an organization formed in
Jerusalem a few years earlier: Yad Vashem, Israel's official
"Remembrance Authority of the Disaster and Heroism."
The book was to be printed in Israel, where costs of production were less than those in the United States. The Israelis
wanted $10,000. If Columbia University Press allocated
$5,000 from its Ansley reserves, said Dr. Friedman, the ac-
quisition of the remainder might not be so difficult. The
Press was receptive to this idea. The imprint of Yad Vashem
might attract the missing funds. Mr. Wiggins left me with
little doubt that he meant Jewish funds.

When I consulted the copyright law I discovered that the importation of books by Americans printed abroad was limited, but I was in no position to set conditions. In April 1958 the entire manuscript arrived in Jerusalem. Yad Vashem's answer was written on August 24, 1958. The complete text of the letter is as follows:

Dear Professor Hilberg,

Your manuscript on the extermination of the Jews has been read in the course of the last two months by several of our staff, each of whom is an expert in one of the aspects involved.

At a meeting of the editorial board which took place on the 15.8.1958, a joint readers' report was considered. In this report it was stated that while the manuscript possessed numerous merits, it also had certain deficiencies:

1. Your book rests almost entirely on the authority of German sources and does not utilize primary sources in the languages of the occupied states, or in Yiddish and Hebrew.

2. The Jewish historians here make reservations concerning the historical conclusions which you draw, both in respect of the comparison with former periods, and in respect of your appraisal of the Jewish resistance (active and passive) during the Nazi occupation.

On the basis of what has been said, our foundation cannot appear as one of the publishers without running the risk that expert critics who know the history of the Nazi catastrophe thoroughly and possess a command of the languages of the occupied states in question, might express hostile criticism of the book.

On the other hand we are prepared to act as mediators between the University of Columbia and the printer here, in order to make possible the book's appearance under the auspices of the Columbia University.

Yours faithfully,
[handwritten signature]
Dr. J. Melkman
General Manager

Here was the first negative reaction to my manuscript, and these bullets were fired at me from Jerusalem. For ten years I had imagined that the Jews, and particularly the Jews, would be the readers of my work. It was for them I labored. And now this. I knew very little about Yad Vashem, and at the time I knew nothing about Dr. Melkman, though I wondered who he was. As I learned later, he had arrived in Israel in 1957. Before the war he had been a teacher of Greek and Latin in a secondary school in the Netherlands, and during the German occupation his Zionist connections enabled him and his wife to hold on to a precarious privileged position, first in Amsterdam, then in the transit camp of Westerbork, and finally in Bergen-Belsen. In writing his letter to me he clearly relied on his staff. To discover the source of his argument about "resistance," I merely had to glance at Yad Vashem's letterhead, which proclaimed the parity of the disaster and heroism. Next to that ideological statement, I could see only an attempt at parochial self-preservation. Did his experts really believe that their Yiddish or Hebrew sources had altered the basic history revealed by the German documents? Could they really stand on the "primary sources" in the languages of the occupied countries when in fact these materials were largely inaccessible to the public and therefore unexplored by Yad Vashem itself? Where were the publications of these experts? Where was the evidence of their expertise? Dr. Melkman did not question the qualifications of his associates, but in referring to my work he permitted himself the use of the phrase "certain deficiencies," knowing that I would have to share his letter with Columbia University Press.

At this point I knocked down the negotiating table, answering Dr. Melkman in a manner that diplomats call "frank." Wiggins was startled by the tone of my remarks. Unlike me, he still harbored a spark of hope that Jerusalem would change its mind. I did not believe in and no longer cared about such a possibility. Nor was my appraisal mistaken. Thirty-seven years later Dr. Melkman wrote to the Hebrew newspaper *Haaretz* that Yad Vashem's decision had been the right one.

In New York the Press's next step was the submission to an outside reader of "portions" of the manuscript segment that followed the pages already judged worthy of the Ansley Award. On December 29, 1958, Wiggins sent me word of the reader's judgment. The crucial sentence in that letter was the following: "The reader felt that the sections 'contained a good deal of important and well documented material,' but thought that many of your comments were more like those of a 'polemical prosecutor' than of an historian and felt that it was impossible for such comments to appear in a scholarly work to be published under the Press imprint."

Was I now accused of indicting the Germans? The anonymous reader had indicated that the manuscript would require "extensive revision" before it would be suitable for publication. Under the circumstances, Mr. Wiggins wrote, the Press could only offer me a contract for the fragment on a take-it-or-leave-it basis. I knew I was going to leave it. How could I find a publisher for the publication of the segment that constituted more than three-quarters of the work? I scarcely even asked myself how, if I succeeded against all expectations, I would deal with two editing styles, two indexes, and two books that belonged together but would be sold separately. The whole idea seemed impossible, and the winter day was bleak. In my savings account I had $1,600. How many years would pass before I had accumulated enough money to satisfy a publisher?

I sent the dismal news to Petschek. He replied immediately, "I cannot help the thought that the size of your thesis is the prime and true deterrent for their readiness to publish the whole work." Then he added, "I would like to help you overcome that obstacle, if this is within my means." He wanted to see me soon. When I visited him in New York he promised $10,000, saying that it was a large sum but that he would continue to eat the same breakfast every day.

A friend of Eric Marder, the philosopher Hilary Putnam, suggested that I send the manuscript to Princeton University Press. I did so without mentioning Petschek's backing. If at all possible, I wanted to walk without financial crutches. Princeton's reply, dated March 25, 1959, and signed by Gordon Hubel, was rapid. It was with "great disappointment," Mr. Hubel said, that he had to report that my study would not be published there. My manuscript did not "constitute a sufficiently important contribution as a case study in public administration to stand alone on that ground," and "readily available" books, such as those of Reitlinger, Poliakov, and Adler, existed "in sufficient detail for all but a very few specialists."

The Adler mentioned by Hubel was H. G. Adler, who had written a major work in the German language about the Theresienstadt ghetto. The book was published in Germany in 1955, but it has not appeared in English translation to this day.

After I received the letter I called Hubel to ask him whether the decision would have been different if he had known that I had backing in the amount of $10,000. There was a moment of silence at the other end of the wire before he answered that Princeton University Press did not act on the basis of financial considerations.

While the manuscript was still at Princeton, an anthropologist at the University of Vermont, John Teal, who specialized in Eskimos and Indians of the Arctic region but who was housed in our department, talked with me about the University of Oklahoma Press. One of the attractions of that publisher, he said, was the physical quality and beauty of its printing and bindings. Since I did not know where to turn, I wrote to Oklahoma, mentioning at the outset the availability of $10,000 for the purchase of books. The University of Oklahoma Press held my manuscript for sixteen months. The editor, Savoie Lottinville, was warm and friendly, but it was almost six months before he received the most excellent reports about my manuscript from his readers. It was a very large one, after all. He then wanted $10,000 as an outright grant. The edition, in a printing of 1,650 copies, would generate costs of $24,000, and at a list price of twenty dollars yielding a net of twelve dollars to the Press, that kind of subvention was needed to recover Oklahoma's investment. Later Lottinville revised the cost estimate to $28,000 for a printing of 2,500 copies, of which 2,000 could be sold, and demanded $17,000 with an offer to rebate a part of the contribution to the extent there might be a surplus.

I was increasingly perturbed. Frank Petschek had had a stroke, and I was corresponding with his son-in-law, Maurice de Picciotto, who undertook to conduct all the foundation's negotiations in selfless labor. Like all university presses, the University of Oklahoma Press did not accept author's funds, but it was prepared to collect money from my university, and the University of Vermont was willing to transmit in its own name any amounts that I could contribute. My savings had reached $3,100. Since my credit with my mother and father was sound, I could borrow the remainder from them. I explained that situation to Mr. Petschek. Sitting in his chair, barely able to speak, he wrote the entire amount, $17,000, on a sheet of paper and handed it to me.

That was still not the end. Savoie Lottinville requested a list of all the organizations to which the Petschek Foundation might recycle the hypothetical rebates. During a one-hour meeting in New York, Lottinville questioned me closely about my background and said that my passages about Martin Luther might offend religious groups. Since the University of Oklahoma Press was not merely a university press but the press of a *state* university, he said, these passages might have to be changed. In the interest of impartiality, he also hinted at modifications of unsuitable comments I might have written about cardinals and rabbis. I said that if he had any specific editorial suggestions, I would listen to them. At the same time I called his attention to the headlines proclaiming Adolf Eichmann's capture by Israeli agents in Argentina. There would be a trial, I said, and we would be missing an opportunity if we did not take advantage of this development with timely publication. Lottinville did not seem to listen. A few months later he demanded the power to make any and all editorial changes, whether or not I approved of them.

During the early stages of my dealings with the University of Oklahoma Press, I talked casually with a representative of Random House, Charles Lieber. He visited the University of Vermont not only to sell textbooks for adoption in courses but to solicit manuscripts. I told him that I had not written anything for classrooms, that my subject was the destruction of the European Jews, and that I was negotiating with the University of Oklahoma Press. While we stood outside my building in the gentle October sun, I also mentioned the sum of $10,000, which Mr. Petschek had already pledged to finance the book. "For $10,000 I will hand-print it for you," he said. "Done," I replied, half playfully, half seriously. As we walked up the stairs, Lieber had second thoughts. Wait, he said, Random House was not really the kind of company that would publish my work. I showed him the carbon copy of my manuscript. "It looks Germanic," he announced, glancing at my footnotes. They were actually brief, but there were thousands of them. The right publisher, he decided, was Alexander Morin, a good friend of his who had been managing editor of the University of Chicago Press and who was now the president of a new, small, independent publishing company in Chicago, Quadrangle Books. He was willing to talk to Morin right from my office if I paid for the telephone call.

Eleven months later I sent Morin the manuscript. He was enthusiastic, full of admiration for my work, and—dispensing with outside readers—he accepted $15,000 of Mr. Petschek's money in payment for copies that were to be shipped as donations to libraries. Before long he sold printed sheets for another $2,900 to a British publisher and obtained an advance order, amounting to a few hundred dollars, for books I would present to my family and friends.

Later I learned that his production costs were only about $18,500. In short, he had recovered the entire investment before publication, and he still had several thousand copies, priced at $14.95 each, which he could sell to the general public. Later his successor, Melvin Brisk, told me that the Petschek Foundation's subvention was not really needed. Most of the books sold to the foundation for free distribution to libraries would have been purchased by these libraries in any case.

To contain his expenses, Morin made some compromises. I did not expect lavishness, and I did obtain all the essentials: the tables, the maps, and the placement of the notes at the bottom of the pages. Nevertheless, I could not help noticing the cheapness of the paper and the binding, which seemed to be an announcement that the book was not made to last. I was pained by the appearance of Table 87, which became Table 87A and Table 87B. The original table was a flow chart, which I had drawn to show the disposition of the last possessions of the Jews who had been transported to the death camps. This chart was not merely an illustration accompanying a case study of public administration, but a portrayal of involvement. It was important to me to encompass in a single drawing all the German offices that had processed these Jewish belongings, and all the categories of people who had been designated as the recipients. I remember working an entire month on the chart, drawing crisscrossing diagonal lines in black and red to replicate this complex of operations and to reflect the mentality of the participants. In my naiveté I assumed that my table would be preserved intact, that it would be a foldout chart in the book. By the time Alexander Morin had completed his surgery, the overview was gone, the clarity obliterated. He had created two half-tables, printed back to back, and my diagonal arrows had given way to horizontal and vertical lines, some of which were formed into rectangles—confusing, incomprehensible, useless.

Morin also chose a double-column format, which irritated me. Many more words were hyphenated; spaces between sections were reduced; and there was an appearance of crowding on the page. After asking me whether I would like black for the cover, he chose brown.

The book jacket was a special problem. I could not help

comparing it with the mantle of the phenomenally success-ful ten-dollar volume on the rise and fall of Nazi Germany by William L. Shirer. Like that best-seller, my book was decked out in white, black, and yellow, albeit in different proportions. Both books were fitted out with swastikas. It seemed that my publisher was trying to ride the Shirer bandwagon. I was slightly, ever so slightly, depressed by this thought.

V
Aftereffects

The Thirty-Year War

In 1985 DAVID WYMAN, the author of *The Abandonment of the Jews*, reviewed the second edition of my book in the *New York Times*. In that discussion he remarked that the first edition had received little notice from the wider public. Again, in 1989, Judith Sklar came to a similar conclusion. As president of the American Political Science Association and a professor at Harvard, she had been invited to lecture at the University of Vermont. On that occasion she said to me that books must appear at the right time, and that *The Destruction of the European Jews* had been published too early.

Topics may be suppressed or catapulted to public attention, but always for reasons that reflect the problems and needs of a society. In the United States the phenomenon now known as the Holocaust did not take root until after the agonies of the Vietnam War, when a new generation of Americans was searching for moral certainties, and when the Holocaust became a marker of an absolute evil against which all other transgressions in the conduct of nations could be measured and assessed. For Germany the time did not come until the 1980s, when the perpetrators were either dead or in old-age homes, and when for the first time their sons and daughters, grandsons and granddaughters, could openly ask questions about the activities of their elders during the Nazi era. In France, a complicated country where former resisters lived next door to former collaborators, time had to pass as well. In both Germany and France decades passed before my work was translated, but then the reception exceeded my expectations.

In the days when the first edition appeared, in 1961, I could sense a general unpreparedness for my subject. I was already aware of realities in the literary world. I was prepared for the difficulty of a small publisher trying to sell a large book. That much was clear to me. What I had not anticipated was the *nature* of the reactions I received, what it was that reviewers accepted as a matter of course, and what aroused controversy.

I had thought my fundamental thesis would become a critical issue. After all, I had asserted that the process of destruction was bureaucratic, that for its successful completion it fed upon the talents and contributions of all manner of specialists, that a bureaucrat became a perpetrator by virtue of his position and skills at the precise time when the process had reached a stage that required his involvement, that he was a thinking individual, and that, above all, he was available, neither evading his duty nor obstructing the administrative operation. This all-encompassing readiness, which had to be deep-rooted, carried certain implications for the question of what Germany was all about. Given the prevailing notion that the Nazis had imposed their will on an unwilling German population, and that the whole regime was an aberration of history, I was braced for a protest: the resurrection of the old emphasis on the role of seducers, deceivers, henchmen, and sadists in Nazi Germany, and the reaffirmation of the essential goodness of ordinary people the world over. Yet there was hardly any objection to my description of the machinery of destruction. Most commentators simply bypassed my analysis or considered it a matter of course. One of them thought about it more deeply and, treating it as a discovery, said that after reading my book he could never see the Final Solution in its old light. That reviewer was Hugh Trevor-Roper.

Trevor-Roper, a wide-ranging historian who refused to barricade himself behind a "Maginot Line" of highly concentrated subject matter, became Oxford University's Regius Professor of Modern History after writing a heavy work about Archbishop Laud and a popular, accessible book about the last days of Adolf Hitler. He also crafted several dozen masterful essays, many of them reviews of books or based on books. Here too, most of his topics were people, like Machiavelli, Sir Thomas More, Gustavus Adolphus, or Karl Marx, but also congeries of individuals, like the Jesuits of Japan, the Quakers, and the Jews. About Jews he had published three essays, one of them in the magazine of the American Jewish Committee, *Commentary*. It must have been Trevor-Roper's book about Hitler and his essays on Jewish subjects that made him *Commentary's* choice as a reviewer of my book. His essay about my work was eight thousand words long, and for anyone who could not muster the energy to read my eight hundred double-column pages, he provided a summary, guide, and evaluation of my findings. His grasp was total, and he wrote more about my volume in another, different review in the *New Statesman,* where he made the crucial observation that the destruction of the Jews was a "national act," and that "disguise it as they may, the Germans were involved in it as a nation."

National character analysis is not pursued in the United States as in Europe, where several writers like Ernest Barker and Salvador de Madariaga have explored this domain. In the United States one treads lightly in matters of national traits, so much so that the principal works about *American* national character have been written by Europeans, like Alexis de Tocqueville, Gunnar Myrdal, or Denis Brogan. In the main, therefore, American reviewers who saw clearly and accepted unequivocally what I wrote about the participation in the destructive labor of German diplomats and soldiers, lawyers and accountants, policemen and clerks, stopped short of attempting to draw ultimate conclusions. For practical purposes I had ignited no controversy about Germany.

The quiet, however, was shattered when Trevor-Roper, whose interest encompassed also the Jews, noticed my description of the actions of the victims during the catastrophe. I had included the behavior of the Jewish community in my description because I saw Jewish institutions as an extension of the German bureaucratic machine. I was driven by force of logic to take account of the considerable reliance placed by the Germans on Jewish cooperation. I had to examine the Jewish tradition of trusting God, princes, laws, and contracts. Ultimately I had to ponder the Jewish calculation that the persecutor would not destroy what he could economically exploit. It was precisely this Jewish strategy that dictated accommodation and precluded resistance. Trevor-Roper now called special attention to my discussion of that topic. He saw immediately that from 1933 to the end, the Jewish leadership was not a new oligarchy installed by the perpetrators, that Rabbi Leo Baeck had been the Jewish leader in Germany before 1933, that the administrative tasks performed by the Jewish councils in German-dominated Europe relieved the German apparatus of a burden, that Jewish resistance was negligible and German casualties almost nil. The active role of the Jews in their own destruction he called the "most surprising revelation" and, prophetically, "the least welcome" to my readers.

And so it was. In *Commentary* itself, Professor Oscar Handlin of Harvard, whose specialty was immigration, including Jewish immigration to the United States, wrote an entire article as a rebuttal to my argument. The title of his essay was "Jewish Resistance to the Nazis," and its tone was set in one of the opening paragraphs in which he referred to my interpretation as an "impiety" that was "defaming the dead." The Jews did resist, he went on, but since he did not wish to "exaggerate," he would point to the fact that collaboration was a general European phenomenon. As to "that awesome moment at the edge of a grave," he found that there, in the final extremity, the victims could comfort themselves with the thought of God's magnificent creation.

After the appearance of Handlin's comments, and a small flood of letters supporting his views, I still thought such reasoning would collapse of its own weight. My assessment, however, was mistaken. The fragile nature of the objections hurled against me did not impair their durability. I had underestimated the importance of myths and had placed too much reliance on soberness. I had not reminded myself enough of Franz Neumann's words: "This is too much to take." The opposition did *not* die. Even in 1993 an article appeared in the German mass-circulation magazine *Der Spiegel* replete with many of the disapprobations I had read in the intervening decades. Added to the repetition of these charges was the accusation that in my subsequent writings I had reiterated and elaborated what I had first said in 1961 about compliant Jewish reactions to destruction. I had waged a thirty-year war against the Jewish resistance.

The author of this article was Arno Lustiger. He was not a professor but an Auschwitz survivor who had become a businessman in postwar Germany. I first met him in 1984 when he introduced himself to me on the occasion of my first public lecture on German soil. He asked me whether the name Lustiger was familiar to me. Yes, I replied, the archbishop of Paris was a Cardinal Lustiger. It was his cousin, said Arno, and he wanted me to know that unlike his cousin he had not converted from Judaism to Christianity. I refrained from complimenting him, but I could not help asking myself, What is he doing in Germany? Is his residence in that country after his Auschwitz experience not as radical a step as the conversion of his cousin in France? Did not both of them achieve success, the cousin as a prince of the Catholic church and he as a potentate in a sector of German business?

There were but fifty thousand Jews in Germany in 1993, and few of them were professors. The criticisms advanced by Lustiger would not be offered by a non-Jew in the German Federal Republic. They were an internal Jewish matter but of considerable interest to the German magazine, which printed them as a one-time opportunity and which hoped to arouse a "controversy," just like the one that had lasted so long in the United States.

It has taken me some time to absorb what I should always have known, that in my whole approach to the study of the destruction of the Jews I was pitting myself against the main current of Jewish thought, that I did not give in, that in my research and writing I was pursuing not merely another direction but one which was the exact opposite of a signal that pulsated endlessly through the Jewish community. This message has three elements, and I had countered all three.

To begin with, there is an insistence that the major effort of Jewish learning and remembrance must be focused on the Jews, *their* circumstances and *their* experiences. Placing the victim rather than the perpetrator at the center of attention is the cornerstone of virtually all the edifices—be they encyclopedias, institutes, or museums—which have been created in the United States or Israel. The largest, most imposing effort is the United States Holocaust Memorial Museum in Washington. I have been associated in minor ways with the creation of this museum. The building is the work of a genius, the architect James Ingo Freed. It has towers and an atrium that recall the watchtowers and parade ground of a concentration camp. During its construction a member of the German federal legislature, the Bundestag, privately expressed the fear to me that *this* building would represent Germany in the heart of the American capital. In the end, however, his concern was too great.

Nestled between other buildings by virtue of its placement in an available space, and limited in height and the choice of materials by government restrictions, it can be seen clearly for what it is only from an aircraft or a helicopter. Once inside the newly opened museum, the visitor was invited to draw a card showing a photograph of a victim. During the walk through the museum halls the person on the card was a constant companion. Indeed, this silent attendant became more familiar along the way as the card was inserted into machines which printed out more information about the victim's fate. Among the exhibits, the visitor could see mounted photographs of an extinct Jewish community, a Gypsy cart and violin, a Danish rescue boat, and many other reminders of the victims' lives. What then about the perpetrators? What may be seen of them?

I had planted the idea that the museum should house a German railroad car in which Jews had been transported to their deaths, and the Polish government actually donated a freight car that had been left on Polish soil. Here then we had obtained a large product of German manufacture, but the exhibitors provided a structural addition for a second perspective. A bridge was built through the open door of the car, so that the visitor may peer into the dark interior and imagine the Jews locked in. I had also proposed that we ask the Polish government for a can of Zyklon gas, with which the Jews were killed in Auschwitz and Maydanek. I would have liked to see a *single* can mounted on a pedestal in a small room, with no other objects between the walls, as the epitome of Adolf Hitler's Germany, just as a vase of Euphronios was shown at one time all by itself in the Metropolitan Museum of Art as one of the supreme artifacts of Greek antiquity. Instead a whole pile of gas cans donated by generous Polish authorities was heaped in the middle of the floor to be stumbled on and noticed with a downward glance. Finally I had suggested that one wall be covered with the photographic portraits of sixteen or twenty perpetrators, known and unknown, to represent the civil service, the military, industry, and the party. The "Hilberg" wall, as the planners called it jokingly, became a display of the Allied war crimes trials. Some of the perpetrators are still there, but in the role of defendant.

The fadeout of the perpetrator is no accident. One editor who compiled accounts of victims chose a characteristic title for his book. He called it *Out of the Whirlwind*. This practice is the ultimate effect of an admonition in Deuteronomy, where one may find the words, "You shall blot out the remembrance of Amalek from under heaven." It is that tradition which is observed also during the Jewish holiday of Purim, when the Scroll of Esther is read and when children with rattles drown out the name of Haman, who sought to kill the Jews of Persia. Once, at a meeting of the United States Holocaust Memorial Council, I heard a presentation of the director, an Orthodox rabbi, Seymour Siegel, who mentioned Adolf Eichmann and, between commas, added the ritualistic words, "May his name be erased." Then and there I reflected on the countless hours I had spent in archives and libraries, searching for the first names of bureaucrats who habitually signed their memoranda only "Klemm," or "Krause," or "Kühne."

Modern Jews know, like their ancient forebears, the hazard of giving the perpetrators a face, of endowing them with identity and thought, of allowing them a modicum of doubt or regret, of making them human. Remember only what they did. And what have *I* done? I insist on delving into forbidden territory and presenting Amalek with all his features as an aggregate of German functionaries.

The prevailing emphasis on the victims has its corollary in the embrace of Jewish sources. The victims do not have much individuality in German documents. There they coalesce indistinguishably into categories: foreign Jews, Jewish laborers, Jewish children; or into numbers: 20,105 Jews, 363,211 Jews, 1,274,000 Jews. Because I used so many of these materials, Arno Lustiger wrote that I banished all the victims "into the anonymous grave of concealment and forgetting," and that I covered the dead "with the records of the murderers," pouring on the graves the "thousands of footnotes" of my books.

I shall not dwell on the fact that the proponents of Jewish sources have paid relatively little attention to the contemporaneous correspondence of the Jewish councils. These collections, however fragmentary some of them may be, are invaluable indicators of the desperate adjustment strategies pursued by the communities in the wake of strangling German measures. My critics are primarily interested not in those records but in the testimony of survivors. In oral history projects a major effort has been made to interview as many of these survivors as possible. There is, however, a sharp built-in limitation in this undertaking. As an early compiler of such accounts, David Pablo Boder, pointed out, he "did not interview the dead." The survivors are not a random sample of the extinct communities, particularly if one looks for typical Jewish reactions and adjustments to the process of destruction.

In their accounts, survivors generally leave out the setting of their experiences, such as specific localities or the names and positions of persons they encountered. Even when they talk about themselves, they do not necessarily reveal mundane information about their financial circumstances or their health. Ghetto life and the early labor camps are not given prominence. The principal subjects are deportations, concentration camps, death camps, escapes, hiding, and partisan fighting. Understandably the survivors seldom speak of those experiences that were most humiliating or embarrassing, and whereas they may mention their hunger, thirst, pain, and fear, it is precisely in these passages that one confronts the implicit or open dictum: "No one who was not there can imagine what it was like." Only one fact is always revealed clearly and completely. It is the self-portrait of the survivors, their psychological makeup, and what it took to survive.

I have read countless accounts of survivors. I looked for missing links in my jigsaw puzzle. I tried to glimpse the Jewish community. I searched for the dead. Most often, however, I had to remind myself that what I most wanted from them they could not give me, no matter how much they said.

The focus on Jewry and Jewish sources is tied to a third imperative. The Jewish victims must be seen as heroic. The Jews in this pictorialization engaged in resistance, many of them, and in many ways. Arno Lustiger, for example, extends the roster of the resisters by including Jewish soldiers in Allied armies and even those Jews who joined the international brigades in the Spanish Civil War, which ended before the Second World War began. More often the concept of resistance is redefined to accommodate such activities as feeding or hospitalizing people in the ghettos, even if the German overlords permitted these functions as part of the maintenance of the ghetto system before the onset of deportations. And more: In 1968, at a conference at Yad Vashem, Meir Dvorjetski of Bar Ilan University presented a paper on "Resistance in the Daily Life of Ghettos and Camps," and enumerated under this rubric the "Individual Renunciation of Chance to Escape" out of loyalty to relatives and fellow workers, and the "Desire Not to Be an Exception," "The Sense of Family and Going Together to Death." Martin Gilbert concludes his book *The Holocaust*, published in 1985, with a paragraph in which he says, "Even passivity was a form of resistance. . . . To die with dignity was a form of resistance. . . . Simply to survive was a victory of the human spirit."

Active, armed acts of self-defense within the destructive arena have nevertheless remained the centerpiece of a historiography and celebration. That these acts have been magnified and popularized should not be surprising. The image of a resister with gun in hand is comforting. Something that is uplifting can be salvaged from the catastrophe. To resist is not to cooperate with the perpetrator, not to follow his orders, not to be meek in the face of death. In Israel such an elevation of the ghetto Jews has been especially important. Before the founding of the state, the Jews who inhabited Palestine and who called themselves the Yishuv, distanced themselves from European Jewry not only geographically. Tom Segev writes of a "common stereotype that depicted the Exile as weak, feminine, and passive, and the Yishuv as strong, masculine, and active." The native-born Palestinian Jew, called the Sabra, represented an ideal, and the Holocaust survivor its reverse. In Yishuv slang, he states, the survivors were called "soap." Given such sentiments, one may understand why an attempt was made to create a sloganized, equally stereotypical response featuring widespread ghetto heroism.

Needless to say I had a problem with this campaign of exaltation. When relatively isolated or episodic acts of resistance are represented as typical, a basic characteristic of the German measures is obscured. The destruction of the Jews can no longer be visualized as a process. Instead the drastic actuality of a relentless killing of men, women, and children is mentally transformed into a more familiar picture of a struggle—however unequal—between combatants. To the perpetrators themselves, the idea of a Jew as such an adversary was psychologically important. A German mobile killing unit would even invent a Jewish "spirit of opposition" to justify a small massacre, and after the largest engagement between Germans and Jews, in the Warsaw ghetto, the SS commandant, Jürgen Stroop, listed every one of his sixteen dead and eighty-five wounded by name, as if to emphasize the magnitude of his losses. When I was testifying in a Toronto case against a purveyor of literature asserting that a holocaust had not occurred in the first place, I heard echoes of Stroop's report in questions posed by the defendant's attorney. The Germans, he intimated, had acted as the responsible authority in an occupied city when they put down the Warsaw ghetto rebellion.

The inflation of resistance has another consequence which has been of concern to those Jews who have regarded themselves as the actual resisters. If heroism is an attribute that should be assigned to every member of the European Jewish community, it will diminish the accomplishment of the few who took action. When Jewry was threatened with destruction, the independently minded breakaway Jews made a sharp distinction between themselves and all those others who had not joined them. "Do not walk like sheep to slaughter," they said, and they meant every word. After the war, some of them still retained the view they had formed in the days when they faced battle. Yisrael Gutman, who was in the Warsaw ghetto, Maydanek, Auschwitz, and Mauthausen, wrote a five-hundred-page book, *The Jews of Warsaw 1939–1943*, more than half of it devoted to the Jewish underground movement and to the conduct of the fighting. Noteworthy is his estimate of the active Jewish combatants, because it is even lower than my own initial figure, which I based partially on Stroop's report. He refrained altogether from estimating how many casualties this small aggregate of poorly armed fighters had inflicted on the Germans and their collaborators. Rachel Auerbach, who stood at the side of the underground Jewish historian Emmanuel Ringelblum, was at pains to tell me that the public did not understand that, if even a hundred Germans were killed or wounded in the ghetto revolt, the result was a major achievement.

Finally, and perhaps most important, the preemption or

magnification of resistance has obscured the reality of Jewish life in the ghettos and camps. One of the most sophisticated and astute observers of the catastrophe is Bronia Klibanski, who was a courier for the Jewish resistance in the Bialystok area of Poland. In a conversation with me in 1968 she expressed her reservations about the equalization—she used the German word *Gleichschaltung*—between the underground fighters and those who did not fight at all. To her the blending of the two groups was not merely a form of dilution, which blurred the multitudinous problems of organizing a defense in a cautious, reluctant Jewish community; it was also a way of shutting off a great many questions about that community, its reasoning and survival strategy. Jewish history could not be written, she said, before these questions were asked.

For thirty years, between the articles of Oscar Handlin and Arno Lustiger, I was almost buried under an avalanche of condemnations. But just before this campaign began, a noteworthy article appeared in a Yiddish newspaper, which—like the other Yiddish dailies—was read mainly by the elderly, and which was therefore already in decline. Although the Yiddish press had barely mentioned my work, the journalist Aaron Zeitlin, whose father, a Yiddish writer in Warsaw, had been killed in 1942, devoted six paragraphs of his column of February 2, 1962, in *Der Tog—Morgen Journal* to reflections about my conclusions. He spoke of Jewish trust and optimism in history, and said yes, this optimism of ours had always been a cane with two ends—more than once it had supported us, but then it had also brought the worst blows on our heads.

Questionable Practices

WHEN THEODOR ADORNO condemned those who would write poetry after Auschwitz as barbaric, I had a problem. I am, of course, no poet, but I have been a footnote writer. Are footnotes less barbaric? In his column "From Friday to Friday" of February 2, 1962, Aaron Zeitlin, who wrote verse himself, noted with a tone of resignation that the Jewish catastrophe would be fashioned into a catastrophology, an academic field of research, and that nothing could be done about such a development. All that had happened would eventually be documented and written down. Even that which was most horrible would in time become history.

And so I try to nod wisely when poets or novelists step forward with their art, which in its very nature is much less disguised than mine. Nor am I disturbed when popularizers of history excavate the monographs of the footnote writers and, distilling the contents, highlight story and drama for a large reading public. The Jewish historian Heinrich Graetz recognized the distinction between researchers, the *Geschichtsforscher*, and writers, the *Geschichtsschreiber*. Not wanting to abdicate in either capacity, he was both.

There are, however, limits. Those I draw are not necessarily enshrined in law, yet in my eyes they mark out areas of inappropriateness or illegitimacy.

Among the practices that give me discomfort is the creation of a story in which historical facts are altered deliberately for the sake of plot and adventure. I remember a time many years ago when my only diversion in Burlington was going to the cinema. Once I watched a film in which ancient Macedonians fought a naval battle with Romans. I was completely absorbed with the scene when I suddenly heard an agonized critique of a few rows behind me. It came from the chairman of our Department of Classics. My own composure was shaken in a bookstore when I spotted a novel with a glittering cover adorned with a large golden swastika on a crimson background. I opened the book at random and discovered more than a whole page containing my translation of a German document that the author of this international best-seller had lifted from a document book I had compiled. Together with this real record he presented fictional texts of bureaucratic correspondence that he had made up to complete his amalgam of history and fantasy. The reader, however, was not informed that my document was fact and that the other, apparently verbatim passages were the author's inventions.

I realize that the example of the golden swastika is far from rare. The creators of a serious film, *The Wannsee Conference*, which was a reconstruction of a high-level bureaucratic discussion about the Final Solution held in wartime Berlin, also took liberties with the facts. The *New York Times* asked me to write an article about the dialogue depicted in this film, precisely because the ordinary viewer could expect a faithful rendition on the screen of everything that could be gathered about the meeting from documents and testimony. I do not know whether my comments destroyed any chance of a meaningful distribution of *The Wannsee Conference*, but I certainly fired on the makers of the film, giving them no quarter. My colleague Samuel Bogorad of our Department of English thought that my attitude toward artistic works was much too rigid. What, he asked, would I say about Shakespeare?

If counterfactual stories are frequent enough, kitsch is truly rampant. In my small collection of art books is a volume of essays, compiled by Gillo Dorfles, about the world of bad taste. The compendium is richly illustrated, and when I look at these reproductions during a late evening hour, I dissolve in laughter. In my subject, to be sure, I do not regard such examples of the aesthetic spirit as comical. The philistines in my field are everywhere. I am surrounded by the commonplace, platitudes, and clichés. In sculpture, Jewish resistance fighters are memorialized in the center of Warsaw by a large heroic statue in Stalinist style. In poetry I regularly encounter graves in the sky. In speeches I must listen to man's inhumanity to man. In some of my own works, the publishers have added their flourishes on jackets, covers, and title pages. The stylized barbed wire appeared on one of my paperbacks. The publisher of the first German translation of *The Destruction of the European Jews* added a subtitle, *Die Gesamtgeschichte des Holocaust*—The Whole History of the Holocaust, to the oversized double-column volume. When I handed an expanded text of this book to an American publisher it was plainly marked "Second Edition," but when the finished three-volume set was sent to me I discovered that he had changed these words to "Revised and Definitive Edition." The editor of an American magazine solicited a paper I had presented at an academic meeting on "The Role of the German Railroads in the Destruction of the Jews" and unilaterally substituted for this title "German Railroads/Jewish Souls." The first German publisher of a small volume, containing my introduction and documents about the railroads, inserted a poem for which, he said, he had paid good money, describing human beings in freight cars, including children whose eyes glowed like coal. Something else happened to the American edition of Claude Lanzmann's book *Shoah*, which comprises the testimony of his multilingual film, including also my statements. Lanzmann had designed this book so that each subtitle on the screen forms a separate line on the printed page. With this format, which preserves the intonations of the speakers and crystallizes the meaning of their utterances, he achieved a special power. The American publisher, however, believed that his reading public was not receptive to poetry. The lines were run together and the book was reduced to a rhythmless, lackluster prose.

The manipulation of history is a kind of spoilage, and kitsch is debasement. What may be said of both is that they are almost routine. Many historians can give personal examples of such experiences, so that my own are certainly not exceptional. I have, however, had disturbing encounters which are distinctly less common. I have in mind the handiwork of three authors who were sufficiently inspired by the muses to think of themselves as special, one as a narrator of events, one in the role of historian, and one as a philosopher interpreting history. Each of them regarded her specific contribution as a capstone to be placed on the work of others. Each considered her work to be a summation in which everything of importance that had been missed was finally resolved, and each complicated my life in her own special way. Their names were Nora Levin, Lucy Dawidowicz, and Hannah Arendt.

Nora Levin wrote a book called *The Holocaust*, with the subtitle *The Destruction of European Jewry 1933–1945*. The volume of 768 pages was published in 1968 by Thomas Y. Crowell, a firm established in 1834. On the opening page Levin makes a grateful acknowledgment to Robert L. Crowell, "who, in a spirit of bold and generous faith in an amateur writer," originally suggested that she undertake the task of writing the book. In a disarming way she points to her "very limited credentials" and her "very limited resources." She was born in 1916 in Philadelphia, where she lived all her life. With a bachelor's degree in education and another degree in library science she had been a teacher in public schools and had taught English and history in high school before she embarked on her career as an author. After her book appeared, I read a review of it by Gerald Reitlinger in the *New York Times*. "I found myself wading," he wrote, "through oceans of stated facts before encountering a single footnote. Then it became apparent," he continued, "that footnotes were scarce because each had been preceded by long recapitulations from single authors." Finally he said, "I began to notice sentences of my own, then whole paragraphs, slightly altered. No quotation marks, no acknowledgments."

If this is what she had done to Reitlinger, I thought, what has she taken from me? The answer was: even more. Her copying was so pervasive that I soon tired of looking for all the passages that paralleled mine. Crowell never withdrew the book, and neither did Schocken, which distributed *The Holocaust* as a paperback. Schocken did not desist even after I reminded representatives of the house, which contacted me in one matter or another, that there was a problem.

Levin, however, paid a continuing price for her literary activity. She was helpless against a rumor network in which facts were sometimes alloyed with imaginary happenings. On January 29, 1982, she sent me a letter, telling me about a "poisonous tale" to the effect that she had made an out-of-court settlement with me. She asked me whether I had heard the rumor and pleaded with me to deny it in writing, so that she might make copies of my answer for ten or fifteen scholars around the world. Since I had never heard this particular tale, I began to compose a letter, certifying that I had not initiated a suit for copyright infringement against her and that she had not made any payment to me for any damage I had suffered, but then I tired of working on my draft.

Lucy Dawidowicz, born in 1915, held a bachelor of arts degree awarded in 1936 and a master of arts degree earned in 1961. She worked almost all her life for Jewish institutions, and she received quite a few grants from Jewish foundations. Her books were devoted to Jewish subjects. She was a New Yorker, moored to the city in which she was born, and when she served on the President's Commission on the Holocaust in 1978–1979 she was the only member of the group who refused to sign its final report on the ground that a museum commemorating the Jewish catastrophe properly belonged in New York City, not in Washington. Just before the war she had visited Vilna, then a part of Poland, where a Jewish Institute, the YIVO, which devoted itself to Eastern European Jewish history and the preservation of Yiddish, was located. When the institute was reconstituted in New York, she could avail herself not only of its facilities but also the knowledge of its staff. In 1975 she published a 460-page book, *The War Against the Jews*, consisting of two disconnected parts, one about the Germans, the other about the Jews. Upon its appearance, the volume received words of praise, such as "distinguished," "trenchant," and "authoritative."

I approached this book as I would any other in my field. Were there any new facts I should know? Was there any insight I had overlooked? In the first chapter I found an extensive discussion of Hitler's *Mein Kampf*. On the first page the author posed a question, which was just short of an answer, suggesting that Hitler had already formed the idea of a Final Solution, that is, the physical annihilation of the Jews, in the 1920s. Really? The next few chapters, based largely on secondary sources and conveying nothing whatever that could be called new, jumped from topic to topic as though the author were anxious to come to the conclusion of Part I. She arrived there, on page 150, asking another question: Did Adolf Hitler decide on the destruction of the

Jews as early as November 1918? "It is a hazardous task," she said, "to construct a chronology of the evolution of this idea in Hitler's mind." The sparse evidence, she added, would no doubt be inadmissible in a court. Lucy Dawidowicz, I am sure, was careful not to enter courtrooms. She was content to leave testimony in war crimes cases, including answers in cross-examinations, to people like me.

The second part of *The War Against the Jews* consisted of a chapter about Germany's Jews and a number of chapters about the Jews of Eastern Europe, in the main, Poland. The Jewish councils in the ghettos, which she called the "official community," were treated briefly as powerless entities. She allotted more space to institutions not directly controlled by the councils, including welfare organizations, house committees, and the rabbinate, all of which she labeled the "alternative community," and to the resistance movement, which she named the "countercommunity." She wrote no chapters about the rest of the European Jews. An appendix, with short, almanaclike entries, took care of them.

I tried not to be mystified by the success of this book. Now and then I glimpsed a semihidden reward for nostalgic Jewish readers. Nothing could really be done, Lucy Dawidowicz seemed to say, not by the Jewish leaders and not by anyone else. Indeed, she reserved her approval mainly for the soup ladlers and all those others in the ghettos who staved off starvation and despair as long as possible. In the end, she observed, everyone was carried away by the tide, including those young men and women who were fired by "the medieval virtues of Christian chivalry" to offer physical resistance. Perhaps such a book was bound to be produced and, given its vaguely consoling words, could easily be clutched by all those who did not wish to look deeper.

In a free market there is a place for every idea and for every product. Yet Lucy Dawidowicz was not wholly satisfied with her rewards. She wanted preeminence. Now that she had spoken, there was no need for other efforts. Hers was the ultimate word. She became a critic, weighing the contributions of researchers and dispensing judgments, some of which she sprinkled into her footnotes. In 1982 Harvard University Press published an entire book of her views, *The Holocaust and the Historians.* I read a discussion of this work in the *American Historical Review* by Henry Friedlander, a survivor of the Lodz ghetto and Auschwitz, whose knowledge of Holocaust historiography was probably unmatched. Friedlander noted some authors of monographs whom she had omitted or dismissed. The list included Poliakov, Reitlinger, and me, as well as H. G. Adler, Uwe Adam, Christopher Browning, Gavin Langmuir, Telford Taylor, Henry Feingold, Saul Friedlander, Meir Michaelis, Randolph Braham, Bernard Wasserstein, David Wyman, Leni Yahil, Elie A. Cohen, Josef Wulf, Helmut Eschwege, Hans Buchheim, Heinz Höhne, Adalbert Rückerl, Jozef Marszalek, Alan Bullock, A. J. P. Taylor, Hugh Trevor-Roper, and Franz Neumann.

There are other problems in her book about the historians. In criticizing an interpretation of a document by an English writer, she states that on November 30, 1941, a transport with Jewish deportees went from Berlin to Prague. This kind of mistake is not an ordinary one. It is not the result solely of carelessness, conjecture, or the failure to see a complication. Rather, it is an error of unfamiliarity that *no* historian specializing in the Jewish catastrophe would be capable of making. It is almost the equivalent of declaring that on December 7, 1941, the Japanese attacked not Pearl Harbor but the Panama Canal.

To be sure, Dawidowicz has not been taken all that seriously by historians. I do not recall a single professional conference in which I saw her as a participant. Nevertheless she had standing enough, not only to publish books but to write about them. Evidently in America there were as yet no standards that could enable even an experienced editor to distinguish between her work and the contributions of so many of the people she looked down upon. And that was a troubling thought.

Hannah Arendt, says my agent Theron Raines, is an icon. Books have been written about her, and in the Federal Republic of Germany her name was given to an express train and her face appeared on a postage stamp. She was born there in 1906. Her field of study was philosophy, and her mentors were Martin Heidegger and Karl Jaspers. Twice she had to flee, in 1933 from Berlin and in 1941 from France. In the United States she began to identify herself as a political theorist. Two of her specialties were totalitarianism and revolution. Both were popular concepts at the time. Totalitarianism in particular was a watchword in the United States, as Americans tried to find common denominators between the Nazi Germany they had just helped to defeat and the Soviet Union, their new foe. Naturally I looked at Hannah Arendt's treatise on the origins of totalitarianism, but when I saw that it consisted only of unoriginal essays on anti-Semitism, imperialism, and general topics associated with totalitarianism, such as the "masses," propaganda, and "total domination," I put the book aside. I never met or corresponded with her, and I heard her in public only twice. All I recall from these two lectures is the emphatic, insistent manner in which she spoke.

In 1961 Hannah Arendt covered the Eichmann trial for the *New Yorker* magazine. Judging from her subsequently published correspondence with Jaspers, she left Jerusalem after a stay of ten weeks, just three days *before* Adolf Eichmann's own extensive testimony began.

When I read the second installment of her account in the February 16, 1963, issue of the magazine, I noted a flattering comment about me. Referring to the difficulties the prosecution faced in untangling the labyrinth of German institutions, she wrote: "If the trial were to take place today, this task would be much easier, for the political scientist Raul Hilberg, in his book 'The Destruction of the European Jews,' published in Chicago in 1961, has succeeded in presenting the first clear description of this incredibly complicated machinery of destruction." I could not help fantasizing what she might have added had she suspected that the experts at Yad Vashem, who supported the prosecution with evidentiary material, had already been introduced to my description of this machinery in 1958, and that, such awareness in Israel notwithstanding, I had not even been asked for assistance in the preparation of the trial.

Hannah Arendt's five articles in the *New Yorker* were densely packed with facts. When the Viking Press published her report in book form later that year, as *Eichmann in*

Jerusalem, I looked for footnotes. There were none. On two pages in the back of the book she stated that her chief sources were the transcript pages and other items that had been handed to the press while she was at the trial. Apparently copies of original German documents introduced in evidence were not part of these packages. A revised and enlarged edition of the book, again under the Viking imprint, appeared in 1964. This version contained a postscript in which Arendt noted that a complete record of the trial had not been published and was not easily accessible. Then she wrote: "As can be seen from the text, I have used Gerald Reitlinger's *The Final Solution* and I have relied even more on Raul Hilberg's *The Destruction of the European Jews.*"

Her reliance on my book had already been noticed by several reviewers before the publication of her second edition. Given the extent of her dependence on me, such a discovery was not difficult. Several commentators, however, went beyond the factual terrain and also attributed her opinions to mine. In constructing this linkage, which has persisted for decades, they unfortunately failed to observe two significant differences between us.

The subtitle of Hannah Arendt's *Eichmann in Jerusalem* is *A Report on the Banality of Evil*. That subsidiary title has the rare distinction of being recalled more clearly than the main one. It is certainly a description of her thesis about Adolf Eichmann and, by implication, many other Eichmanns, but is it correct? In Adolf Eichmann, a lieutenant colonel in the SS who headed the Gestapo's section on Jews, she saw a man who was "déclassé," who had led a "humdrum" life before he rose in the SS hierarchy, and who had "flaws" of character. She referred to his "self-importance," expounded on his "bragging," and spoke of his "grotesque silliness" in the hour when he was hanged, when—having drunk a half-bottle of wine—he said his last words. She did not recognize the magnitude of what this man had done with a small staff, overseeing and manipulating Jewish councils in various parts of Europe, attaching some of the remaining Jewish property in Germany, Austria, and Bohemia-Moravia, preparing anti-Jewish laws in satellite states, and arranging for the transportation of Jews to shooting sites and death camps. She did not discern the pathways that Eichmann had found in the thicket of the German administrative machine for his unprecedented actions. She did not grasp the dimensions of his deed. There was no "banality" in this "evil."

The second divergence between her conceptions and mine concerned the role of the Jewish leaders in what she plainly labeled the destruction of their own people. It had been known before, she said, but now it had been exposed "in all of its pathetic and sordid detail" in what she called my "standard work." The whole truth, she said in a sentence that was quoted over and over, was that if the Jewish people had been unorganized and leaderless there would have been chaos and misery, but not between four and a half million and six million dead.

In writing about the Jewish councils I had emphasized the extent to which the German apparatus counted on their cooperation. The accommodation policy of the councils had ended in disaster. For me, however, the problem was deeper. The councils were not only a German tool but also an instrument of the Jewish community. Their strategy was a continuation of the adjustments and adaptations practiced by Jews for centuries. I could not separate the Jewish leaders from the Jewish populace because I believed that these men represented the essence of a time-honored Jewish reaction to danger.

In Israel itself there had never been a splitting of the Jewish councils from the ghetto Jews in general. During the early years of the Jewish state, the victims were still considered to have been trusting and weak individuals. As late as 1957, only a year before Dr. Melkman's letter rejecting my manuscript for the way I treated this history, *Yad Vashem Studies* featured an article by Benzion Dinur, Yad Vashem's chairman, who stated in unvarnished language that the councils could not be considered in isolation because they constituted an "expression basically of what had remained of the confidence Jews had in Germany even under the Nazi regime." The Jews, he said, "carried out regulations" even if they could have evaded them at some risk to themselves. In the Netherlands they had "hurried with their luggage" to the trains that would carry them to the east, and "even in Warsaw and Vilna, in Bialystok and Lvov, reports of death journeys were discredited for a long time."

Dinur's train of thought had not completely disappeared in Israel when the Eichmann trial began; the view was maintained by Israel's youth in particular. When Jewish survivors testified about their experience publicly in the court proceedings, the issue was therefore joined. It was the witnesses who were on trial. If they could not explain their behavior to the new generation, the old image would be confirmed and they would be judged to have been automatons. To the dismay of Hannah Arendt, the prosecution asked several of the survivors *why* they had followed orders. Thus the attorney general: "Dr. Buzminski, you knew it was a death train, didn't you? Why did you enter these cars?" The witness, as it happens, had jumped out of the train, but the questions remained, and now the repair work was pursued methodically from Jerusalem to New York. The Jews, it was said in metronome fashion, *had* been heroic, *had* resisted, and this assessment covered leaders and followers alike. Not surprisingly, when Hannah Arendt's *New Yorker* articles appeared, the wrath of the Jewish establishment, as she called it, descended upon her and simultaneously upon me.

In March 1963 the Council of Jews from Germany, an international organization of Jewish emigrants from that country, published a statement in the press. Referring to "recent opinions" about the Nazi period, the council declared that a historical picture influenced by such opinions would be a falsified one. "This is especially true," it said, "of the book by Raoul Hilberg which appeared in 1961, '*The Destruction of the European Jews*,' and of the articles published by Hannah Arendt in '*The New Yorker.*'"

Hannah Arendt and I were coupled so often that I could even act as her stand-in. On October 18, 1963, the New York literary critic and political commentator Irving Howe chaired a symposium about "Eichmann and the Jewish Tragedy." He wrote about this event twice, in the *Partisan Review* that same year and again, at length, in his autobiography eighteen years later. In the *Partisan Review* he stated that he and his fellow organizers had invited Hannah Arendt "herself" to speak. "She declined," and so did Bruno Bettelheim, who was invited next as a man whose views were thought to be similar to those of Arendt. "We then asked Raul Hilberg, author of a scholarly volume on which Hannah Arendt leaned." The meeting, he said, was "excited and passionate," but "at no point—I repeat, at no point— was anyone shouted down." In his autobiography Howe described the meeting as "hectic" and "sometimes outrageous," but also "urgent and afire."

My own impressions were slightly different. When I was invited to this symposium I was told in writing that I would have thirty minutes to speak. I knew I would have difficulty with such a time frame, but I did not wish to reduce the scope of my topic. I was still thinking of dealing with Eichmann *and* the Jews, a combination that was almost unmanageable.

The hall in the hotel was filled with hundreds of people. One of them was the poet Robert Lowell. I asked him why he was present at such a gathering and he replied, "I've got to be where the action is." So this was going to be spectacle. On the dais Irving Howe informed me that I would have just twenty minutes. I was not adamant enough to demand the half-hour I had been promised, and I was not experienced enough to throw away my prepared thoughts immediately, to assess the audience before me, and to address it directly. I had come with transcript pages of the Eichmann trial, and I read from the testimony of a woman who had lived in a primitive village of Volhynia, and who was herded

153

with her family to the edge of a mass grave where her young daughter asked her why they did not flee. The impatient guard had asked whom he should shoot first, and he shot the child. The mother, wounded, dug herself out of the grave. *This* is a scene, I wanted to say, that illustrates what happens when orders are followed. *This* was the outcome of Jewry's age-old policy. I was not friendly. I did not yield, and I was oblivious to the fact that I was tearing open unhealed wounds. I was not allowed to finish. A panelist pounded on the table with his fist. His banging, magnified by the microphone, was followed by a cascade of boos. Irving Howe invited the audience to ask questions and make comments. Now one after another individual rose, one to accuse me of sadism, another to read from a prepared written statement challenging my figures on the German dead in the Warsaw ghetto battle, and so on, on and on.

In later years I have given hundreds of public lectures. A few times I was honored with standing ovations, but I will not forget that particular evening in the seedy New York hotel.

When Hannah Arendt wrote her postscript to the second edition of her Eichmann book, she had grown bitter. It was not she who had claimed "that the Jews had murdered themselves." The "well-known" construct "ghetto mentality," which she attributed to the Israelis and which, she pointed out, had been espoused by Bruno Bettelheim, was not hers. Then she said that "someone who evidently found the whole discussion too dull had the brilliant idea of evoking Freudian theories and attributing to the whole Jewish people a 'death wish'—unconscious, of course." But who was *that* individual? When I first read these lines, I could not solve this riddle. I simply did not know anyone who wrote or spoke about death wishes in connection with the Jewish fate. More than twenty years passed before I read Arendt's correspondence with Karl Jaspers. On March 24, 1964, he asked her whether I had defended her. She wrote back on April 24:

> I have heard nothing about Hilberg taking my side. He is pretty stupid and crazy. He babbles now about a "death wish" of the Jews. His book is really excellent, but only because it is a simple report. A more general, introductory chapter is beneath a singed pig. (Pardon—for a moment I forgot to whom I am writing. Now I am going to let it stand anyway.)

The correspondence was published by Piper Verlag in Munich in 1985. The American translation, which appeared in 1992, did not contain the sentence with the words "stupid" and "crazy." Curious, I inquired about this omission and was told that the statement was struck on legal advice.

In the 1960s Piper Verlag was much more concerned with libel than in 1985. When that publisher considered her *Eichmann in Jerusalem* for the German market, the possibility of lawsuits became a stumbling block. In the absence of footnotes, her multitude of statements about a great many living individuals, most of them in Germany, were unsubstantiated. Struggling in a four-page letter, dated January 22, 1963, with answers to Klaus Piper's detailed questions, she said at one point:

155

Here as elsewhere I have used material presented in the book by Raul Hilberg that appeared in 1961. That is a standard book, which makes all the earlier investigations, such as those of Reitlinger, Poliakov, etc., appear to be antiquated. The author has worked for fifteen years only with sources, and if he had not, in addition, written a very foolish first chapter, in which he shows that he does not understand much about German history, the book would have been perfect so to speak. No one at any rate will be able to write about these things without using it.

I found this letter among her papers in the Manuscripts Division of the Library of Congress. Coincidentally, in that same collection I also unearthed a letter addressed to her on April 8, 1959, barely four years earlier, by Gordon Hubel of Princeton University Press. In that letter I discovered that the press had turned to *her* for an evaluation of my manuscript. Thanking her, Hubel enclosed a check. Here then was the source of Hubel's argument—which he invoked in rejecting my work—that for all practical purposes Reitlinger, Poliakov, and Adler had exhausted the subject. This assessment was Hannah Arendt's thinking a year before Eichmann's capture in Argentina.

I still wonder what triggered her reactions to my first chapter. Was she really aroused by my search for historical precedents, such as the roots of anti-Jewish actions from 1933 to 1941 in the canons of the Catholic church, or the origin of the Nazi conception of the Jew in the writings of Martin Luther? To be sure, she had a personal need to insulate the Nazi phenomenon. She went back to Germany at every opportunity after the war, resuming contacts and relationships. With Heidegger, who had been her lover in her student days and who was a Nazi in Hitler's time, she became friendly again, rehabilitating him. But in dismissing my ideas she also made a bid for self-respect. Who was I, after all? She, the thinker, and I, the laborer who wrote only a simple report, albeit one which was indispensable once she had exploited it: that was the natural order of her universe.

VI

What Does
One Do?

The Second Edition

I N 1948 I HAD CHARTED A COURSE that I pursued heedless of my prospects. In 1961 I had no course. Rudderless, adrift, I waited. By 1963 I was tempted by an opportunity to extend my research. My publisher in Chicago, Quadrangle Books, employed a literary agent who tried to sell *The Destruction of the European Jews* to European publishers. In Munich the Droemersche Verlagsanstalt Th. Knaur Nachfolger bought the German rights and made arrangements for a translation. The library of the University of Vermont had obtained an English transcript of the Eichmann trial, and I could not resist reading its six thousand mimeographed pages. I purchased microfilm copies of those trial documents that I had not yet seen in my research. This small augmentation and a few other items I weaved into the book for the German edition. It was work for one and a half summers, plus the free hours between them. I sent the insertions to Munich in July 1964.

I traveled to Europe after mailing the package. Germany was not a country I wished to visit, but I stopped in Munich for one day on August 24, 1964, to meet with anyone at the publishing house who could see me, and if possible to talk with the translator about any problems.

When I arrived at the hotel I was met by a Droemer/Knaur representative who was not my editor and who professed to know nothing about the progress of the translation or any other publishing plans. He did not invite me to the offices of the company but to a coffee house. I remember nothing of that casual conversation other than his remark, which I took to be deliberate, that he was partly Jewish. Then I left immediately.

It was not until June 1965 that word came from my editor at Droemer/Knaur, Fritz Bolle. "If you have not heard from us in so long," he wrote, "it is because we have been preoccupied again and again with the difficulties of publishing a German translation of your work." It was not my documentation that was the issue but my thesis of Jewish—and here he used quotation marks—"collaboration." After long reflections and thorough discussions, the company had decided that a German edition could have "very dangerous consequences," because malevolent people could pose the question, "But why have the Jews collaborated? Why did they not resist?" and could draw anti-Semitic conclusions from such questions. "That there are malevolent people, you know," he said. "That they can be dangerous, we know." A newspaper like the neo-Nazi *Die Deutsche Nationalzeitung*, he said, could create much damage and poison the atmosphere.

I could not take Fritz Bolle's arguments very seriously. From newspaper reports I knew that hundreds of trials for National Socialist crimes were being prepared in Germany and that there was opposition to these proceedings. One prosecutor had written to me in 1962 and again in 1964 to inquire whether a German translation was in the offing. He said that he had been asked about this matter again and again by his colleagues. I could imagine that my book might be a tool in the hands of a prosecutor and that a publishing house responsible for its distribution in the German language could arouse the ire of all those who sympathized with the defendants. At the time I could think of no other pertinent reason why Droemer/Knaur, which had already paid an advance to Quadrangle Books, would take the serious step of breaking a contract.

To be sure, there were Germans who might have read my book nostalgically, admiring their incomparable Final Solution. They might conceivably have looked in the index for their names, nodding. Such readers could also have considered the Jews who surrendered themselves and their families to be despicable. What they would never have done, however, is to share their feelings with anyone publicly. The *Deutsche Nationalzeitung* did have a respectable circulation in Germany—it was sold openly in kiosks—but that paper was not likely to say that the Jews failed to resist the honorable German army, SS, or police; it would brand me, as it did on March 3, 1967, as the "standard Zionist author," and it would describe the destruction of the Jews as the "Lie of the Six Million."

The "malevolent people" did not suddenly appear in 1964 or 1965; there were at least as many of them in 1963, when Droemer/Knaur made the contract, as two years later. Yet something to which I paid little attention did happen in the interim: the appearance of the German version of Hannah Arendt's *Eichmann in Jerusalem*. On August 7, 1964, just before my visit to Munich and the publication of Arendt's book, Paul Arnsberg wrote a long article in the *Rheinischer Merkur* about the reactions to her work in the United States, calling the debate the "Affair Hannah Arendt." In her correspondence with Jaspers, she wrote on September 24, 1964, that her German publisher Piper—like Droemer/Knaur in Munich—had just told her that some booksellers were actually boycotting her *Eichmann in Jerusalem*. The store owners had informed Piper that they did not *want* to sell the book.

Here then, after all these years, I had found a kernel of truth in Bolle's letter. Jewish accommodation and cooperation, which Bolle called "collaboration," *had* become a problem, because taking Ms. Arendt's side or mine in the "controversy" was to risk offending a significant segment of the Jewish community worldwide.

My short-lived relationship with Droemer/Knaur did not upset me. Without a full understanding of the tortured thinking in the offices of German publishers, I saw only a concern for former perpetrators. Many a practitioner of the Nazi era was still at his desk in the Federal Republic of Germany, and every forty-year-old had lived through that time.

But the failure in Munich did underline my isolation. No institution of higher learning in the United States was really interested in research about the destruction of the Jews. I already knew by 1963 that I would be staying in Vermont for the rest of my career, and I solidified that situation when, newly married, I bought a house, the one in which I still live. My house became my refuge. From my rear windows I look out at nothing but trees, which are green in the summer and completely covered with the pristine white of snow in the winter. Here, gradually, almost imperceptibly, the decades rolled away.

In 1965 I closed my eyes to my subject, but then, a few years later, I resumed my search for documents. Again, I took advantage of an opportunity. This time no friendly stranger had deposited a collection in the university library. I had to look for new materials elsewhere. The possibility was created by the University of Vermont, which had abolished sabbatical leaves during the Great Depression of the 1930s but reinstituted the practice in the more prosperous 1960s. A waiting list of old-timers in the faculty preceded me, but my turn came in the spring of 1968. With paid leave for six months, I could travel to archives abroad to examine records that had never been brought to the United States. I began to think about the gaps in my book, particularly the role of the German railways and the relatively unknown death camps of Belzec, Sobibor, and Treblinka. The place to explore these topics was Germany, but I could not imagine living there with my small family even for a few months. I chose, instead, Jerusalem, in which the Yad Vashem archives were located. This was a mistake.

For an entire month I was not allowed entry into the archives. Clearly I was persona non grata. Literally knocking on one door after another in the administrative building, I was given all sorts of explanations and advice. The chairman of Yad Vashem was out of the country, said one of the staff members, and nothing could be done in his ab-

165

sence. I should have written for permission before coming, said another. Since I was already in Israel, said a third, I should go to the oral history archives in Tel Aviv, where access was unrestricted. In Tel Aviv I spent several weeks examining statements of survivors. Then I went back to Yad Vashem where I met the remarkable Bronia Klibanski.

During the war she had been at the side of Mordechaj Tenenbaum-Tamaroff, a young man who had tried to organize resistance in several ghettos and who was killed in the short battle of the Bialystok ghetto. She must have studied languages, for—as she told me—she could read all the materials in her archives except those in Hungarian. She had never written much, despite her insights into the dilemmas of the Jewish population under German rule in Poland, and she had a subordinate position at Yad Vashem, categorizing records and, I believe, using her linguistic skills and her noble, graceful gestures to conduct important visitors to various exhibits in the place.

When we first met, I introduced myself: "My name is Hilberg." "You—you are Hilberg!" She began to laugh. On her own, violating the rules that had been recited to me, she allowed me to sit in the archives, from which her superior, Josef Kermisz, did not eject me. Very few staff members exchanged any words with me, and it was some weeks before I discovered that after six years my book had been reviewed in the latest volume of *Yad Vashem Studies*. The review was thirty-six printed pages, and its title was "Historical Research or Slander?"

In later years I visited Yad Vashem again. I was even invited to be on one of its editorial boards and to deliver a paper on Jewish councils. In 1968, however, I was wrestling with problem after problem: my inability to find an apartment in crowded Jerusalem, the hours spent on buses commuting from Tel Aviv, and the limited hours when the archives were open. As I contemplated ruefully the meager yields of my research, I decided to give myself a short time in efficient German archives, which were not barricaded for my arrival and which held significant collections. The time in Germany was too short, and I was returning to Vermont with a diversity of materials which did not constitute a coherent whole.

I was in my forties, and for men in America this particular passage through life was known by the title of a popular novel as the "hurricane years." It was the age at which a man might face unexpected misfortunes or reverses. He might experience a sign of mortality, like a heart attack, or a failure in his career, like a lost appointment or promotion, or the collapse, as in my case, of a marriage. At such a time of disequilibrium and disorientation, the organism seeks reflexively a new stability on a secure plateau, salvaging its remaining resources and possibilities.

During my absence from Burlington in the spring of 1968, my colleague Jay Gould had unwittingly provided me with a psychological base. He had seen to it that I was elected to a small university committee that passed on all reappointments and promotions of faculty members. A year later I was also elected to the chairmanship of a faculty committee that was charged by the university's board of trustees with seeking a new president, it being understood by several key members of the board that the winning candidate should be a white native-born man of a Protestant denomination. Finally I was appointed to the chairmanship of my department. The university absorbed me almost completely. I studied it in all its characteristics: its administration, faculty, and students, the sources of its revenue, and the allocation of its funds. In this microcosm I was simultaneously a participant and observer, fascinated, buoyed. And then I stopped.

In the spring of 1976 I had another sabbatical leave. This time I went straight to archives in Germany and Austria. It was clear to me that I was returning to my documents, but I was not sure what I would do with them. In 1969 and 1970 I had spent late evening hours in my study, translating some of them for a small compilation which Quadrangle Books published. In the later 1970s I imagined an enormous expansion of this initial exercise, a multivolume undertaking. In my reveries I thought of myself as commander-in-chief of a project that would employ researchers and translators, all of them working on items under my supervision, producing a storehouse in the English language of materials gathered from archives all over Europe. The selection, organization, and explanation of these documents would be my contribution. The dream spurred me to look wide and far. When I testified in courts for the governments of the United States, Canada, and Australia, I was strongly motivated by the prospect of obtaining any new evidence these governments could obtain through official approaches to the Soviet Union, where archives were still closed to the public. When I joined the President's Commission on the Holocaust and its successor, the United

States Holocaust Memorial Council, I lobbied for the creation of an archive that would be filled with microfilms of pertinent records from European archives. Considering the heavy emphasis of the council and its museum on the oral statements of survivors, it is a veritable miracle that an archive was established for documents and that such collections were filmed in the Soviet Union, East Germany, and Romania. A document project of the kind I had in mind for the benefit of future researchers in the United States was, however, the sort of investment that—even if vanishingly small in comparison with the cost of a museum—would have been considered an unjustifiable luxury.

There was only one remaining possibility. The documents I was collecting enriched my knowledge. With them I could fashion a description that would be more accurate, complete, and incisive. In short, I was moving toward a second edition of *The Destruction of the European Jews*. From a practical point of view the proposition was nightmarish enough. Revisions of monographs are not welcome ventures for publishers. If the first version was a failure, why try a second? And if, as in my situation, the original edition could be sold in modest, predictable quantities continually, why spend the money for a new one? I had to work steadily while remaining poised for any opening, domestic or foreign. Eventually these opportunities did arise, and I produced, if translations are counted, second, third, and fourth editions. Each time I inserted new material painstakingly into a preexisting text. No other approach was feasible, inasmuch as I had to respond to developments when I encountered them.

Because I was not the master of my fate, I was tense, often on edge. Of necessity, my eyes were simultaneously fixed on my documents and publishers. The publishing world, in turn, seemed to be in turmoil, and starting with Quadrangle Books it presented me with surprises. By 1971 Quadrangle had become a house that stood for high quality. By dint of effort, the second president, Melvin Brisk, and his capable young editor, Ivan Dee, had built a list of some three hundred respected titles. That year the New York Times Company bought Quadrangle. A few years later Quadrangle (now Times Books) sold some eighty of its titles, which were deemed "textbooks," including my first book and the new document volume, to a publisher of children's literature, Franklin Watts. To me this transaction was so bewildering that I visited an editor of Times Books in New York and asked him why I had been sold without so much as a letter explaining the action. When I talked with this man I became aware that he had been associated with Irving Howe and I suspected that he had been one of the organizers of the symposium in the Diplomat Hotel. The editor did not really answer my questions, but I remember him saying that Times Books would publish "other good books."

For the first time I realized what the grant of a right to print really means. It could be passed on and the author's work might be nothing but a commodity in the hands of total strangers. Franklin Watts sold the two books for several years until they disappeared from *Books in Print*. I called Theron Raines, who had become my literary agent, and he advised me to engage a lawyer for the purpose of regaining the rights to my book. Soon I was free again, and

Raines sold the rights for a five-year period to Harpers, so that I could work purposefully on a second edition. My only remaining problem was the total lack of interest in such a project on the part of publishers everywhere. Theron Raines began to talk about the need for a sizable subvention, and I had a sense of déjà vu. After all these years, the subject was still in limbo.

I did not even think about a translation into German. In 1967 a friend of a friend had suggested my work to Rowohlt, a major publisher near Hamburg. The answer, by F. J. Raddatz, was that Rowohlt was already "burdened" with nonfiction and that my book would mean the abandonment of several literary works. In 1979 a much smaller company, the Verlag Darmstädter Blätter, inquired about the book but then decided it could not manage publication financially. A literary agent in Switzerland wrote to Raines on March 5, 1980, that C. H. Beck, an old established German publisher specializing in legal commentaries, had turned down the book as well. "You will not unload more than 600-800 copies," the agent wrote. "I doubt whether more than 20 people would read the edition. It is far too long."

In Germany, however, members of a new generation were coming to the fore. They were born during or after the war. One of them, from a family of railroad men, was a publisher of railroad books. His typical readership consisted of people who were interested in timetables of the Trans-siberian railway during tsarist times. He found out about my study of railroads in the Nazi era and in a daring move offered to publish a documents book with my commentary about the trains that transported Jews to their deaths. That small book, which appeared in 1981, was the first German publication with my name on the cover.

Before the close of 1980 I received a letter from a small West Berlin publisher, Olle & Wolter. This firm wished to publish my large book. Ulf Wolter, who corresponded with me, was in a hurry, and in 1982 I went to Germany frantically researching material for last-minute inclusion in his edition. While there I became curious about this man. Why did he want to bring out this work, which apparently no one else in Germany would touch? Seeking an answer to this question, I boarded a plane to Berlin to meet him.

He was a young man whose family had managed to cross into West Berlin from East Germany just before the wall cut off escapes. Like several of his friends, he was a bachelor. His office was in an inconspicuous building reached through a courtyard. The space was cavernous but inexpensive. He prided himself on spending very little money for rent. That is why, he explained, his costs were considerably lower than those of his larger competitors. To prove his point he quartered me for the night in a pension where one had to switch on the hall light, which went out automatically before the guest had found the room. I had almost always chosen modest accommodations on my research trips, but this time I felt uncomfortable. Perhaps because the pension occupied an upper floor of an apartment house, perhaps because of the stairs of stone, the sounds, the cell-like nature of the room with its 1930s furniture, I imagined the brown-shirted SA downstairs and men in boots ascending the steps and banging on doors.

The next day I asked Wolter why he was publishing my book. His list had given me no clue. He had been interested in a translation of a work by one of my University of Vermont colleagues, the Sovietologist Robert V. Daniels, who wrote about the Trotsky deviation from communist orthodoxy, and I had spotted titles by radical or socialist German authors as well as books by feminists. By why mine? Wolter, who had mastered English, said he had read my book while still in college and had decided then to publish it in German translation as soon as he had established himself as a publisher. His books, he said, were centered on one theme: injustice. He could not have omitted mine.

I was impressed by Wolter, even though he had rushed me much too much, and I was impressed by the masterful translator to whom he had introduced me, Christian Seeger, another young bachelor. I asked Seeger why so many young men I encountered in publishing and journalism had not married, and he answered that he himself had several siblings and that there were enough Germans in the world.

At this point I was also on the threshold of another edition in the United States. Discouraged, I had not been looking for a publisher, but a very small house that I had never heard of asked me to evaluate a manuscript, and after I had done so, the owner, who turned out to be a survivor, asked me what I was doing. I am reasonably sure he did not expect the answer I gave him, but he was not fazed. I in turn was attracted by his choice of titles and the mode of his publication. He had never had a best-seller, he said almost with pride, but he chose good acid-free paper as well as fine designs for covers, and in keeping with such devotion he had never remaindered a book. What he did not tell me is that he would charge an unheard-of price for my three-volume set and that he regularly denied a standard trade discount to distributors. Thus he would be mailing these sets direct to libraries and private purchasers, deriving a relatively large profit from very small sales. He died, but the book languished, comatose, in his publishing house.

This new American edition, which I labeled the second but which was really the third and which he had restyled "revised and definitive," appeared in 1985. By then I had invested a great deal of work in it, splicing the additions seamlessly into the text so that a new reader might see no vestige of the old limits. In this endeavor I had succeeded only too well, for now most of the reviewers did not notice most of the augmentations either. For Lucy Dawidowicz the three volumes were sheer bulk in any case: a sign of my inadequacy as a writer. I was consoled, however, when, on the other end of the scale, Christopher Browning, the highly sophisticated researcher who had explored a wide range of subjects pertaining to the Jewish catastrophe, found every significant insertion and highlighted it in his review.

Not until 1988 and not fully until 1992 did I realize that I had become a European author. In 1988 a major French publishing house, Fayard, brought out the book. The contents were further expanded—my fourth edition. No doubt Fayard had become interested in the project after the showing of Claude Lanzmann's film *Shoah*. Unquestionably the success of the book was assured by the efforts of my young editor, Eric Vigne, who combined intelligence and sensitivity with driving energy. In addition, the subject was new in

France, and books still mattered there. "Do not forget," my American publisher said in self-defense when I compared his dismal sales performance with the success in France, "that there your book is a first edition, and do not assume," he added, "that the two markets are at all alike." Finally, however, I knew that in France the time had come, for Lanzmann's film, for Vigne's talents, and for my work.

In Germany, Ulf Wolter became ill, and his publishing company disappeared. Yet even this marginal entrepreneur had sold more copies than anyone would have thought possible when he asked for my book. In 1990 S. Fischer Verlag, a major publisher in Germany, produced a three-volume set—a second edition in Germany—in paperback. "We will lose money," my editor, Walter Pehle, predicted. But he found a donor, Dieter Dirk Hartmann, who enabled him to cover some of the costs and to lower the price of the published work. In the end the book became a commercial success.

Again and again I went to Germany to lecture and be interviewed. The Germans probed deeply, not only into the contents of the work but also its genesis. How had I begun? Why? In particular, they wanted an answer to a mystery that troubled them especially. They seldom phrased the problem succinctly or posed the question outright, but once, in Berlin, a young person asked simply, "Why did we do it?"

The Diary of
Adam Czerniakow

D O YOU KNOW WHAT WE HAVE?" The rhetorical question was put to me by Josef Kermisz, the archivist of
Yad Vashem, at the end of my stay in Jerusalem in the spring
of 1968. He was a short, slightly built man, and his tone
suggested that despite his small physical stature and his subordinate status in the organization, he was in a position to
grant or deny access to documents in his custody, thus holding the direction and success of outsiders' research projects
in his hands. "What do you have?" I asked, playing his
game. "The diary of Adam Czerniakow," he answered.

His words had the desired effect. I remembered immediately that in the 1950s Jacob Sloan edited the diary of Emmanuel Ringelblum, the Warsaw ghetto historian who had
been seized and killed after going into hiding. Sloan had to
use a sanitized version that had been published in Warsaw,
because he was not given permission to view the original
Ringelblum diary in Warsaw or its copy in Jerusalem. The
Sloan edition was consequently published without crucial
passages in which Ringelblum had mentioned the Sobibor

death camp and had asked why the Jews went like sheep to the slaughter. Josef Kermisz was the jailer of the Jerusalem copy. Yet Kermisz did have a problem. He was in the position of all those who have a secret but who cannot impress anyone with their power unless they divulge it and thereby relinquish their monopoly and indispensability. In the case of the Ringelblum diary, Kermisz solved his dilemma by inserting the missing fragments on special yellow pages in a volume of *Yad Vashem Studies,* thus calling the attention of specialists to his treasure while still not allowing a revised edition of the stunted English translation ten years after it had appeared. What would now be done with the diary of Adam Czerniakow? To my mind, that diary was likely to be of even greater importance than the writing of the ghetto historian, because Czerniakow had been chairman of the Jewish Council of the Warsaw ghetto.

"If you have a diary by Czerniakow," I said slowly, deliberately, "then you should publish it in the United States." Oh no, not so fast, Kermisz answered. The diary was an extremely complicated text, he said, and required commentary by experts before it could be published. And in what language, I asked, would the diary appear? In Hebrew, of course, Kermisz answered.

I was already familiar with the argument that I was to hear for another twenty-five years—"We Israelis have the expertise; you Americans have the money"—but for the moment I could do nothing. I was leaving Jerusalem, not really sure I would ever return. Yet I could not forget this conversation after my departure. I had never seen such a document. Whatever its contents, it was bound to answer many questions. What was it like to be a ghetto leader? What sort of individual was Czerniakow? The diary was his private record, the scarcest kind of account altogether.

Several years passed before I learned that the diary had been published in an obscure Polish journal—the same publication of the Jewish Historical Institute in Warsaw that had printed the censored diary of Ringelblum. Since the original Czerniakow diary was in Polish, one had only to make sure that the transcription was complete and correct before using it for any purpose. Then I discovered there were two Hebrew editions, and that one of them contained the facsimiles of Czerniakow's handwritten pages next to the Hebrew translation. With a magnifying glass, one could discern the Polish words.

Although I could not undertake a translation into English myself—Polish was yet another important language I had not studied—I had a colleague, Stanislaw Staron, who came from Poland. It was he who had brought me a copy of the Polish journal after one of his visits to Warsaw. I looked at the format of the diary. Virtually every entry began with a notation about the weather. Clearly this piece of literature would not be a best-seller. It was a Pepys kind of diary, Staron announced. I was undeterred. This document had to be translated, studied, and explained, and Stanislaw Staron was the ideal man to accomplish these tasks.

Stan, as he liked to be called, was a highly sophisticated man. His field was political theory, and for his dissertation topic he had written on the Neo-Thomist thought of Jacques Maritain. When I read his dissertation I was taken by its lucidity. For the first time I became fascinated with a manuscript about theories that I would under no circumstances have examined myself. Staron was absorbed by their structure, symmetry, and balance, though he admitted to me that his analysis of Maritain had taken too long. "I should have chosen a simpler topic," he said to me. "Like what?" I asked. "Like 'Freedom,' for instance," he answered.

Staron, however, was also a man of the world, with an understanding of the world. He liked to ski, a sport I never appreciated at all. He lived in Scotland, where he had begun to admire British culture, but he remained the quintessential Pole and a hopeless romantic who never married. Once he met Bronia Klibanski, with whom he was completely enchanted. "Raul," he said, "it is a pity you cannot hear for yourself what beautiful Polish she speaks." Stan was in uniform from the first day of the Second World War to the last. He did not wish to be praised, and so, in describing him, one must recite only the simplest facts of his wartime life, which began with the German invasion of Poland and his capture. He escaped—"It was easy," since many Poles had accomplished this feat—and was brought by a Polish underground organization via Hungary, Yugoslavia, and Italy to France, where he joined a Polish division. After the German offensive in the west had broken through the Maginot Line, and British forces had retreated to Dunkirk, the officers and men of his division were told: Every man for himself! Staron and several thousand other Poles streamed to the French port La Rochelle (from which I had left Europe a year earlier in peace). On a blacked-out unarmed troopship they sailed for England, and Stan Staron spent the next few weeks as an artillery officer with something like Napoleonic cannon on the Scottish coast awaiting the Germans. Three years and eighteen practice parachute jumps later, Staron was on the Continent again. When the war ended he was fighting in the Netherlands. Like many Poles in his position, he could not go home, and after pursuing his academic studies in Scotland and the United States, he eventually came to Vermont. Here he devoted himself mainly to investigating Communist Poland's political institutions, particularly the relations of church and state. Always he was hemmed in by his own self-limiting rules. One must not write about this or about that. One must not be a traitor to Poland. One must not and must not.

I broached the question of the Czerniakow diary to him. It was an ideal venture, I argued, knowing that he would never write more than his well-crafted articles about the Polish political system. Yet he would not touch the text without my participation. Very well, we would work together. I already knew of microfilms containing records of the German city and ghetto administrations in Warsaw, which would be invaluable for our introduction, the notes, and an appendix. These films, made by the Jewish Historical Institute in Warsaw, had been delivered to Yad Vashem in exchange for a typewritten copy of the diary. It was that copy from which the Warsaw institute had printed the Polish text.

I also knew of an editor who would be interested in our project. In 1970 Benton Arnovitz, who worked at Macmillan, had written a blind letter to me, asking whether I would be interested in undertaking a study of half-Jews under the Nazi regime. The subject, I replied, was very important, but

I could not exploit it beyond the stage I had already reached in my book. Then, with an unfailing scent of what had to be written, he suggested Jewish councils. I replied that to my knowledge, Isaiah Trunk had prepared a manuscript on that subject in Yiddish, and that it was languishing in his drawer. Arnovitz published this pathbreaking study in English translation. It was not a popular work, but it received a National Book Award. Arnovitz later explained that the publication of such a heavy book had been possible because Macmillan "owed him one." "How so?" I inquired. Arnovitz pointed out that Macmillan was the publisher of the memoirs of Albert Speer, the man who had been in charge of Germany's armaments production during the Second World War. Trunk's work served to redress the political balance. Obviously, however, Trunk was no match for Speer in the book market, and Arnovitz was still interested in any manageable manuscript I could deliver. At this point I mentioned the Czerniakow diary, even though the diary assuredly would not be a fount of major profits.

Benton Arnovitz was a man of strong convictions. He had served in the United States Army as a reserve officer, eventually with the rank of lieutenant colonel, and he was not loathe to use the word "honor." He was also one of the best editors I ever had. His knowledge of books, my subject, and the market, was matched by his concern for authors and their expectations. He had a strong aversion for the city of New York, which is the capital of the American publishing industry, and when he moved, just to be away from the metropolis, we moved with him, to Chilton of Philadelphia, a house known for automobile repair manuals, and then to

Stein and Day of Briarcliff Manor, which filed for bankruptcy while the diary was still in print.

When I had suggested the diary to Benton Arnovitz, I considered it to be in the public domain. That was not the view of Yad Vashem, which asserted a copyright to the document. At one point a publisher engaged by Yad Vashem demanded that Arnovitz suspend publication "as promptly as possible." Then the two publishing houses agreed to cooperate, but with provisos, dictated by Yad Vashem, one of which, as summarized by Arnovitz, stated: "Hilberg's footnotes must be factual, identified as his, and under no circumstances can be evaluative." When Yad Vashem's publisher decided not to be involved in the project anymore, Arnovitz invited Yad Vashem to join us. Thus the cover of our edition of the Czerniakow diary featured Kermisz as one of the editors, and his separate introduction was included as well. All this required the good offices of Herman Wouk, the novelist, and Yehuda Bauer of the Hebrew University, as well as the dedication of Benton Arnovitz.

Our cooperation with Yad Vashem was remarkably smooth. I especially appreciated the work of Yad Vashem's specialists in identifying numerous Jewish personalities, many of them obscure, whom Czerniakow had mentioned in his entries. All the notes were merged and distilled to their essence. There was resistance in Yad Vashem in only one small matter. Benton Arnovitz wanted illustrations, and the archives of Yad Vashem did not wish to furnish any photograph showing Jews in factories working for the Germans. It was not a totally insignificant omission, considering Czerniakow's daily efforts to increase production in the ghetto.

By the mid-1970s the chairman of Yad Vashem was Yitzhak Arad, a former partisan in Belorussia and a retired general of the Israeli army, who also held a doctorate and who had written several valuable books, one of which, about Vilna, I used as a text in my course. Arad struck me as intelligent, plain-speaking, and purpose-oriented. Unfortunately I could not always deal with him personally. When an opportunity arose later to publish the diary in Germany, the vice-chairman, Reuven Dafni, was incensed that I had responded to the inquiry without deferring to Yad Vashem. In a "how-dare-you" kind of letter, he reiterated the assertion that "Yad Vashem had full copy rights" to the diary. I had never met Dafni, and not realizing that I was addressing a ranking diplomat deserving of all the courtesies due such a person, lectured him about copyright and taunted him with the question whether Yad Vashem's acquisition of the manuscript was the sort of transaction that could sustain a claim to ownership. I withdrew from the German edition, which was eventually published by Beck without my name and without explanatory apparatus save for a minimal introduction by Yisrael Gutman and a handful of notes. But I wished to impress upon Dafni that, whereas Yad Vashem had possession of Czerniakow's original notebooks, one of which was still missing, it had yet to show that the property had been acquired from someone whose ownership of the book was indisputable.

The "chain of custody," as lawyers refer to a document passed from hand to hand, troubled me from the beginning, and I repeatedly demanded that, so far as known, the successive possessors of the diary be identified in print. Josef

Kermisz had been evasive about this matter in conversation, but in his introduction he disclosed that in 1964 the Israeli embassy in Canada had purchased the diary from a woman, Rosalia Pietkewicz, and that she in turn had bought it from an unknown source in 1959. Stanislaw Staron, who traveled to Canada frequently, had already talked with someone who remembered reading about the transaction in the newspapers. But who was Rosalia Pietkewicz? From whom did she obtain Czerniakow's notebooks? I looked for her address in telephone books—we even wrote to a priest with the same last name—but then we learned that once she had been Rosa Braun, that she was a Jewish woman who had hidden outside the ghetto, and that she had left Poland with the diary in the 1950s. Stan Staron even managed to interview her in Canada. "Well?" I asked after his return. "Did you find out how she got hold of the notebooks?" Staron, the gentleman, had been an able artillery officer, but he was no interrogator of women, and when Rosa Braun did not offer an explanation spontaneously, he did not press her for an answer. In Jerusalem, where I pursued my inquiry without letup, I was told that she had offered the notebooks to the embassy for $100,000, claiming risks and expenses she had incurred, and that after lengthy negotiations the embassy had offered $10,000, which she had accepted.

Although I wanted to learn all the details of the diary's fate, if only because they were a part of Czerniakow's biography and the ghetto's history, I was never in doubt that the notebooks were genuine. I needed no tests of paper or ink, and no samples of Czerniakow's prewar handwriting, because a reading of even half a page convinced me that no

184

one could possibly have made up such a manuscript with its wealth of references to specific occurrences and people.

Staron invested his entire background and personality in the work of translation. He approached it like a consummate musician examining a score for the first time. He played this text with all his training and restraint. His translation was artless, unadorned, translucent. When I read it, page after page filled me with suspense. The diary became a place, a strange locality that I was entering for the first time. I was a voyeur, a ghost inside Czerniakow's office, unobserved, and the longer I inhabited that enclosure, the more I saw.

My first and foremost impression was that Czerniakow knew, even while Warsaw was still under German siege in September 1939, that he was living through a time when every moment was significant. This consciousness penetrates each of his entries. He recorded events perseveringly, scarcely ever omitting a day, no matter how crowded his schedule or how wearisome his experiences may have been, and his entries were always factual, as if he had split himself into two men: the leader of the largest Jewish community on the European continent in his official functions, and the detached observer in his writings. He was almost sixty when he became chairman of the Jewish Council, viewing the scene with the eyes of a mature man, and because he stood at the interface between the German overlords and the Jewish population his vantage point was unique. The ghetto wall marked a sharp separation between perpetrator and victim, but Czerniakow was like a bridge. With him I crossed the boundary, as he went out to hold his difficult official conversations with Germans and as he returned de-jected to the Jewish world. I dwelled with him to grasp his struggle with problems of housing, food, starvation, disease, taxes, and police, and to observe him while he had to listen to the incessant wailing of Jewish women beseeching him for help outside his office door. On the day when the diary was published in the United States, I believed that we were opening this vista to a larger public. At that crucial moment Lucy Dawidowicz wrote her negative review in the *New York Times,* belittling the diary and for good measure drip-ping acid on me, Professor Staron, and the University of Vermont.

One surprise in the diary was going to interest very few readers. Czerniakow, representing a community of 400,000 people, had met only once with the governor of the Warsaw District, Ludwig Fischer. Similarly, he had recorded only one conversation with the Gestapo chief of the district, Walter Stamm. By contrast he would talk repeatedly to some SS sergeant, and several times he would meet with a German functionary so low in rank that only diligent re-search in microfilms enabled us to establish the fact that this individual was also one of the official overseers. What had Czerniakow been reduced to? For the welfare of his people he depended on appeals, explanations of needs, and argu-ments. And to whom could he direct his entreaties? Some-times he did not even know who would listen to him when he made his rounds to talk to clerks and functionaries who were half his age. One scrutinizer of the diary, who also no-ticed the subordinate status of the individuals in the Ger-man control apparatus, was Albert Speer. The former Reich minister of war production, however, looked at the phenomenon from the opposite vantage point. What struck him was the sheer delegation of power over the largest ghetto in Europe to such petty underlings.

How did Czerniakow retain his composure? He ate his ghetto soup and looked at a reproduction of a Watteau on his wall. He also made jokes. Once, he referred to himself as the king of Croatia. Another time, visiting a Jewish asylum for mental patients, he was accosted by an inmate who asked him whether he was Czerniakow. No, came the reply, he was not. In the matter of a typhus epidemic, he likened the effectiveness of Jewish physicians to that of rabbis. I recall giving a talk to several hundred functionaries of Jewish organizations in San Francisco, and I thought that these men and women might like to hear about an organization man from another time and another place: Czerniakow. In my summary I recited some samples of Czerniakow's humor. The audience sat stunned and silent.

I spent about six years with Czerniakow. The more I delved into the diary, the more I discovered there. What was it that drew me to this man? He had a sense of honor, of not being allowed to desert his post. He soberly noted his foreboding about the Jewish fate. Without an intelligence organization of any kind, relying only on chance remarks by Germans, veiled newspaper accounts, and ever-present rumors, he anticipated the bitter end. When the deportations began, he wanted to save the Jewish orphans, and when he could not secure even their safety, he killed himself.

I was immersed in Czerniakow's life when Claude Lanzmann filmed me in Vermont. I told him about my work, and Lanzmann had me speak about the man and read from the diary. At the end, Lanzmann said to me, "You were Czerniakow."

The Triptych

IN THE SUMMER OF 1961 I spent a month in Europe, traveling from country to country, from city to city, and from museum to museum. In the museums I found silence. The sculptures were silent. The paintings were silent. I studied the portraits in particular: here a youth, there an old man, a cardinal, a pope, but also peasants and soldiers. All were mute and all were dead, but at the moment they were close to me. Why did I dwell in these museums? At the time I did not know, but now I realize that I was reaching for a new conception, that then and there I had found a model for a book I would write twenty-five years later, *Perpetrators Victims Bystanders*.

All my life I had been preoccupied with organizations. I constructed organization charts and charted the flow of decisions. Now I looked for the people: individuals and groups. The images were in my mind, and I wanted to paint them, in words of course, but in such a way that they would remain portraits, to be absorbed in an instant just like a canvas that is seen at a glance.

When the perceptive German historian Eberhard Jäckel reviewed the book in its German translation, he juxtaposed

189

it with my first book. In this comparison he saw something highly unusual: I had written about the same subject, but I had produced a completely different work. In my earlier effort, he said, I had been influenced by my mentor Franz Neumann. If Neumann's *Behemoth* was the classic description of the German Nazi system, then *The Destruction of the European Jews* was the *Behemoth* of Jewry's annihilation. Now I had evolved from Neumann in that I dealt with individuals. Jäckel's observation was true. I *had* stepped out of Neumann's confines, but my departure was also an abandonment of political science. Although I still used what I knew about political systems, I had chosen a medium that was different from the traditional writing of political scientists. My focus was no longer the closed realm of the political decision-making apparatus. I was now posing a question that was at once smaller and larger than my previous quest—smaller, because people as such are not a bureaucratic colossus, and larger, because I wanted to encompass everyone who stood on stage during the Jewish catastrophe. I did not intend to omit any man or woman solely for his or her political insignificance. Adolf Hitler rated a chapter by himself, and other important players might receive at least a paragraph or sentence, but in the overall scheme I strove for parity, and now and then the smallest individual was given equal space.

Furthermore, the perpetrator was no longer the primary factor. Perpetrators, victims, and bystanders were arranged in three groups, and to each I gave much thought in my research and analysis. I kept these groups apart, drawing vertical lines between them, just as they had been separated from one another, physically and situationally, in their life-time. Yet they were linked, despite their distinct experi-ences, by the event in which they were all involved, and which they witnessed simultaneously. In this panorama the reader could select one chapter or another, in any order. For one reviewer, Jonathan Rosen in *New York Newsday*, this in-terchangeability, and my uniform style, created a "disturb-ing sense of sameness."

I was not the first to deal with ordinary people. Christo-pher Browning wrote a book about a German police battal-ion, *Ordinary Men*, which appeared in 1992. John Dickinson talked to 172 persons to recreate the fate of one obscure Jewish victim in Germany. This biography, *German and Jew*, was published by Quadrangle Books in 1967. In the film *Shoah*, Claude Lanzmann dealt with all three personae, and virtually all the individuals who appeared on the screen were small people, none more distinguished than professors and a few who were illiterate. Lanzmann even found most of his interviewees in small places, and these people and lo-calities are shown in a nine-and-a-half-hour mosaic.

When I began to assemble my own cast of characters, I thought the undertaking would be relatively easy. After all, I had been gathering materials for three and a half decades. But it did not take long before I was back in the archives to search with an altogether different perspective for more court records, personnel files, and correspondence, in order that I might provide telling illustrations of different *kinds* of perpetrators, victims, and bystanders. It was not until I had finished the work, in fact not until after its publication, that I fully realized something else.

Most often novelists, journalists, and even historians look for an unusual or bizarre occurrence in a mundane setting, but I was doing the opposite. For me, the destruction of the Jews already was the setting, the irremovable reality, and within this extraordinary outburst I looked for all that was ordinary. I had done so from the beginning, when I dealt with everyday bureaucratic procedures, and now I was pursuing the same object as I examined the lives of people. In their daily routines, these individuals, like agencies, sought stability, particularly their own private equilibrium. It did not matter whether they were perpetrators, victims, or bystanders; they all manifested a need for continuity and balance.

Often enough I had been struck by images of such behavior. Christopher Browning relates in one of his essays that Herbert Andorfer, the Austrian who commanded the Semlin camp near Belgrade, played cards with Jewish women to while away the time, before he received orders to shove these acquaintances into a gas van. In a book of photographs of the Warsaw ghetto, there is a picture of the ghetto elite, in suits and dresses marked with a star, drinking alcoholic beverages. The female bartender leans over the counter to join a conversation of patrons; half-empty liquor bottles can be seen in the background. Yet another compilation of bourgeois scenes is a pictorial work edited by Gilles Perrault and the prominent French historian Pierre Azema, on Paris under the German occupation. There one can see a display of fashion designs by Jacques Fath, Nina Ricci, and Schiaparelli; a young crowd at a swimming pool; and a 1943 photograph of Jean-Paul Sartre sitting in the Café de Flore with a glass of wine, smoking a pipe. Such examples are legion.

The craving for the familiar, the habitual, the normal, emerged as a leitmotif wherever I looked. Psychologically this clinging was aimed at self-preservation, and its manifestations run like a thread through the upheaval. At a basic level they provide an explanation of how these groups managed to go on—the perpetrators with their ever more drastic activities, the victims with their progressive deprivations, the bystanders with the increasing ambiguity and ambivalence of their positions. When Sigmund Freud delivered a lecture about war during the first major conflagration of the twentieth century, he said that mankind needed a passing check from the burdens of civilization. What I began to note was the reverse side of the phenomenon: the adhesion to time-honored products of this civilization in the midst of unprecedented destruction.

In my untutored walks through museums I have been an eclectic. I was riveted to the violence of trench warfare as depicted by Otto Dix, and I was electrified by the luminosity of the fantasies painted by Paul Delvaux. Most of the time, however, I would gaze at masterpieces, known and unknown, of the Renaissance. Once, in the Louvre, I saw a sign: "This way to the Mona Lisa." A coil of people stood in front of that most famous of all paintings, and I, to avoid the crowd, decided not to join it. Glancing to my left, I spotted a quiet portrait that everyone bypassed. Astonished and transfixed, I wondered: Who was the lady in this picture? Who was its painter? Her name was thought to be Lucrezia Crivelli, and she was painted by Leonardo da Vinci.

To be sure, I am not Leonardo, but in the English-speaking world my book *Perpetrators Victims Bystanders* has been bypassed by several cognoscenti who had hailed *The Destruction of the European Jews*. Some American and British critics used words like "short," "petty components," and "a sketch map" in describing my latest work. Since that is all they could see, they rushed on, disappointed, searching for new creations elsewhere.

VII
Vienna

O N OCTOBER 24 AND 25, 1992, a little more than a month after the publication of *Perpetrators Victims Bystanders* and its review in the *New York Times*, I attended a conference in the Chicago area. All those who came, about eighty people, were teaching Holocaust courses in colleges and universities. The purpose of the meeting was to explore how such courses might be taught. I was one of the specialists invited to address the whole gathering.

I had looked forward to this event, hoping to see a display of books and to spend a few hours in a congenial atmosphere with a group of like-minded people. There was no book display, and one of the speakers, Yisrael Gutman of Yad Vashem, who had as yet not read my new book, attacked me with reference to *The Destruction of the European Jews*. After I had spoken about problems of teaching the subject, he asked for the floor again to attack me for what I had said in my talk. The presiding officer was in dread that I would wish to reply to Gutman, but I had no such desire. Despondent, drained, and exhausted, I wanted to banish the last six weeks together with this unforeseen denouement.

On the afternoon of the 25th I boarded a plane again. In

my seat I ceased to think. As the aircraft took off, the ground fell away and so did the oppressive feeling that had weighed me down. The flight was my escape. In the morning I would be in Frankfurt, my initial destination, where the German translation of my new work had already appeared. It was to be the first departure of ten to Germany, or Austria, The Netherlands, Belgium, France, and Italy in the next three years.

During my brief European stays I spoke and gave interviews dozens of times. Almost all the interviewers were knowledgeable. They were interested in the origins of my formulations, and they plied me with questions which were not only personal but also philosophical. Most of the reviews in the newspapers were written by erudite historians and journalists. Moreover, some of these discussions were longer and more detailed than their American counterparts. The historian Hans Mommsen devoted what must have been many hours to his analysis, which he wrote with exactitude and deep understanding. When I compared the initial German and Dutch reviews with those I had received in the United States, I was struck by a clear dichotomy. To verify my impression I sent the German comments to Eric Marder and asked him whether anyone would believe that the Germans were reviewing the same book. He agreed: the difference was startling, whether one looked at the quantity of the German discussions or their quality. After this appraisal I shipped copies of the German commentary to my American editor at HarperCollins, Aaron Asher, for consolation, and to Eric Vigne at Gallimard, where the French translation was still in progress, for encouragement. Vigne sent me a postcard suggesting wryly that Germany needed the book.

I should have known that a work offered primarily to one readership may instead be embraced by another. There is a place as well as a time for books. Still, this development made me reflective. Once, in 1961, a host on a New York radio station asked me whether I boycotted Germany. Yes, I replied. For how long, the interviewer asked me, would I maintain my boycott? Until 1985, I replied unhesitatingly. "Now you sit with us, eat with us, talk with us," said my German editor, Walter Pehle, one late evening when I sat with him, his daughter, and his assistant, at an outdoor table of a Berlin restaurant. "Yes," I replied, thinking that I had found new associations and a new acceptance in a country I had boycotted for so long.

Walter Pehle grew up after the war. He earned his doctorate in history and by 1992 had brought out a veritable library of books about the Nazi period. He liked to travel, and on two or three occasions he accompanied me on lecture trips he had arranged for the promotion of my three-volume paperback and the new title, both of which his company, S. Fischer Verlag, had published. When I mentioned that the Austrians had not been very interested in my work and that I had not set foot in Vienna since 1976, when I pursued my railroad research in one of the court archives there, he made sure that I had a few interviews and a small speaking engagement in that city. He liked Vienna and met me there.

What was I searching for in Vienna? On previous stopovers, and particularly during my stay in 1976, I had retraced the steps of my childhood, taking the walks that I remembered from the 1930s. On all these occasions nothing had impressed me so much as the fact that visually Vienna was unchanged. I saw the same houses and the same stores. Only distances seemed smaller. When I had walked with my father through the major park of the XX. District, the Augarten, it had seemed immense. In 1976 I traversed it in fifteen minutes. The Vienna of my youth had shrunk into a smaller replica of what it had been. Why did I return one more time? What could I find there in 1992? Did I seek encounters? Did I want to hear voices? Did I hope to discover a mirror in which I could see myself as I had been? As I was now?

In the early morning of November 27 I flew to Vienna from Cologne. An interviewer met me at the airport. He told me that a thirty-five-year-old colleague, to whom he had mentioned the planned interview, had exclaimed, "What, again?" "It is the first time," my interviewer had answered him.

Walter Pehle confided in me that Austria was not the very best market for Fischer books about the Third Reich. I was not surprised to hear his statistics. The postwar Austrians had isolated and insulated themselves from history. The shortest *Who's Who* I had ever seen was a 1948 Austrian edition filled with skiers and opera singers. Since then Austria had played the neutrality sonata masterfully, cajoling and beckoning to the foreign tourist. Here I was, a visitor myself, savoring the incomparable Wiener Schnitzel, Strudel, and Topfenkuchen. I could not help admiring the Austrian pronunciation of the German language, which—with its cadence and clarity—can in and of itself be made into a demonstration of perfection. No wonder that Walter Pehle, open-eyed though he was, could be entranced.

"Let me show you my Vienna," I said to him, after he had joined me in the city. "Let me show you the Danube Canal, my old street, and the house I lived in with its stone steps, bereft of hot running water. Let me show you the hidden Vienna."

We walked along the canal to the XX. District. Pehle, who had a camera with him, photographed the Viennese mountains from a bridge. The scene was no longer that of my childhood. A massive tower designed by Hundertwasser intruded upon the view. On the Wallensteinstrasse, which is very short, we reached the old apartment house in a minute. "Here," I said, pointing to the cold-water spigot on the floor, but there were signs of indoor construction. We asked a tenant who walked down the stairs whether she had hot running water. She had. "Come," I said, as we approached the door of my old apartment. This time, fortified by his presence, I rang the bell. I really wanted to see the apartment, to test my memory of its size and layout, to look out the windows. Possibly some of our old furniture was still there. But no one answered. The name, Anna Gruber, was still on the door. Evidently her husband, who had given us the ultimatum on November 10, 1938, to leave the apartment, was dead. Conceivably he had not survived the war. She herself might in the meantime have become ill, and as we stood there she might have been in some hospital. She had certainly not taken an afternoon walk. A notice from one of the utilities was stuck in the door. "We came too late," I said to Walter Pehle. She had lived there for fifty-four years.

In the center of the city I had several more interviews in a coffee house. One of the interviewers, Evelyn Adunka, was exceptionally perceptive and insightful. She asked me about Neumann, Baron, and my father, and she quoted a paragraph from a private letter she had discovered in an archive. The letter was written on March 6, 1962, by H. G. Adler, the survivor of Theresienstadt, who was the author of the massive book about the ghetto. I had never met or corresponded with Adler, who had lived in England until his death in 1988. Reading that thirty-year-old letter, which like all of his books was written in German, I felt as though Adler had peered directly into the core of my being. This is what he said about me:

> To be noted is Hilberg's "The Destruction of European Jewry." Surely you have heard of this work. It is until now the most significant accomplishment in this topic area and it is not likely to be surpassed very soon, even though it is by far not yet the final portrayal. No one until now has seen and formulated the total horrible process so clearly. The number of small errors and omissions do not matter seriously, and so far as I can see, they can be extinguished in a new edition. What moves me in this book is the hopelessness of the author, who was born in 1926, and who came to the United States before the war, surely from Germany to which he returned at the end of the war with the US Army. In 1948 Hilberg began his work. Therefore he already has the

viewpoint of a generation, which does not feel itself affected directly, but which looked at these events from afar, bewildered, bitter and embittered, accusing and critical, not only vis-à-vis the Germans (how else?), but also the Jews and all the nations which looked on. At the end nothing remains but despair and doubt about everything, because for Hilberg there is only recognition, perhaps also a grasp, but certainly no understanding. . . .

Index